MONTGOMERY OF ALAMEIN

EL ALAMEIN TO THE RIVER SANGRO

Few military commanders can have carried
such responsibilities on such a scale, for so
long and with such success, as Field Marshal
Montgomery. This volume is, as 'Monty'
himself writes, '. . . an authoritative account of
the activities of the Eighth Army in the days
of its greatest success.'

El Alamein was the turning point in the war:
from that momentous battle the tide against
Germany turned, and during the time the
Eighth Army was commanded by the Field
Marshal, it lost not one single action.

Montgomery of Alamein is a superb example
of military history presented by one of the
greatest and most well-known generals to
command victorious armies in the field . . .

'This book represents a personal view and
interpretation of great events as seen through
the eyes of one of this country's greatest
soldiers of the 20th century . . .'
—*Journal of the Society for
Army Historical Research*

Montgomery of Alamein

Volume I

El Alamein to the River Sangro

Field Marshal
The Viscount Montgomery
of Alamein
K.G., G.C.B., D.S.O.

CORGI BOOKS
A DIVISION OF TRANSWORLD PUBLISHERS LTD

MONTGOMERY OF ALAMEIN: Volume I
EL ALAMEIN TO THE RIVER SANGRO

A CORGI BOOK 552 09683 0

Originally published in Great Britain
as *El Alamein to the River Sangro*
by Hutchinson & Co. Ltd, 1948

PRINTING HISTORY

Hutchinson edition published 1948
Barrie & Jenkins edition published 1973
Corgi edition published 1974

Corgi Books are published by Transworld Publishers Ltd,
Cavendish House, 57–59 Uxbridge Road, Ealing,
London, W.5.

Filmset in Photon Times 11 pt by
Richard Clay (The Chaucer Press), Ltd, Bungay, Suffolk
and printed in Great Britain by
Fletcher & Son, Ltd, Norwich

**NOTE: The Australian price appearing on the
back cover is the recommended retail price.**

CONTENTS

Acknowledgements   x

VOLUME ONE
EL ALAMEIN TO THE RIVER SANGRO

Foreword   3
Introduction   5

PART I
THE CAMPAIGN IN NORTH AFRICA FROM EL ALAMEIN, 13 AUGUST 1942, TO THE END IN TUNISIA, 12 MAY 1943

1. The Situation in the Eighth Army in August 1942   9
2. The Battle of Alam Halfa, 31 August 1942   13
3. Preparations for the Battle of El Alamein   20
4. The Battle of El Alamein, 23 October 1942   23
5. The Pursuit to the El Agheila Position   46
6. The Actions at El Agheila (13 December 1942) and Buerat (15 January 1943) and the Advance to Tripoli   50
7. The Advance into Tunisia and the Battles of Medenine (6 March 1943) and of the Mareth Line (20 March 1943)   67
8. The Battle of Wadi Akarit (6 April 1943) and the Advance to Enfidaville   89
9. Administration in the North African Campaign   100

v

PART II
THE INVASION AND CAPTURE OF SICILY,
10 JULY–17 AUGUST 1943

10. Planning the Invasion of Sicily   111
11. The Assault on Sicily, the Extension of the
    Bridgehead, and the Advance to the Plain of
    Catania, 10–21 July 1943   123
12. The Completion of the Capture of Sicily   134
13. Administration in the Sicily Campaign   144

PART III
THE INVASION OF THE MAINLAND OF ITALY AND
THE ADVANCE TO THE RIVER SANGRO,
3 SEPTEMBER–31 DECEMBER 1943

14. Planning the Invasion of Italy   151
15. The Assault on Calabria, the Advance to the
    Catanzaro 'Neck', and Development of
    Operations to Potenza, 3–19 September
    1943   156
16. The Development of Allied Strategy in Italy
    and the Advance of Eighth Army to the
    River Sangro   164
17. The Battle of the River Sangro, 28 November
    1943   176
18. Administration in the Campaign in Italy   188
19. My Farewell to the Eighth Army   194

MAPS

The Advance of the Eighth Army   4
1. The Battle of Alam Halfa   14
2. The Battle of El Alamein—23 October–
   3 November 1942   22
3. The Battle of El Alamein—The Plan on 30
   Corps Front   25

4. The Battle of El Alamein—The Break-in and Dog Fight   31

5. The Battle of El Alamein—Regrouping and the Thrust Towards the Coast   37

6. The Battle of El Alamein—The Break-out   41

7. The Pursuit to El Agheila   49

8. The Battles of El Agheila (13 December 1942) and Buerat (15 January 1943), and the Advance to Medenine   49

9. The Battle of Medenine—6 March 1943   68

10. The Battle of Mareth—20 March 1943   79

11. The Battle of Wadi Akarit—6 April 1943   90

12. The Advance to Enfidaville   94

13. The Eighth Army in North Africa—Time and Space   102

14. Operations in Sicily—10 July–17 August 1943   128

15. The Invasion of Italy and the Advance to the River Sangro   166,

16. Battle of the River Sangro   182

Index   *see* Volume III

LIST OF ILLUSTRATIONS

1. 'Donald' was the mascot of the C.M.P.s of the 10th Armoured Division H.Q. He had been 'found' somewhere in the Nile Delta some months before and had been in the desert ever since, 24 October 1942

2. One of the first pictures taken during the battle shows this group of Italian prisoners captured by the Highland Division, 26 October 1942

3. German prisoners of the 90th Light Division captured by Australian units are escorted past an appropriate sign

4. British trucks carrying infantry through a gap in an enemy minefield come under heavy shellfire, 27 October 1942

5. Something for the troops in action to dream about! At their barracks British A.T.S. girls enjoy the luxury of their excellent swimming pool

6. Filling a Crusader tank the hard way with a four-gallon can. Later in the campaign the Allies adopted the 'Jerry-can'

7. This amusing sign in the Alamein lines is not so frivolous as it sounds, 27 October 1942

8. The realities of war in the desert are brought home in this picture of a dead Italian lying beside a Breda gun, 29 October 1942

9. Rather a macabre sign for one of the many blood banks which moved forward with the advance and saved many Allied lives, 29 October 1942

10. The General Priest carries a 105-mm. Howitzer on a self-propelled chassis. It has a high turn of speed and good manoeuvrability and proved particularly

successful against the German 88 mm. anti-tank guns, 2 November 1942

11. One of the great pictures of the war. Australians storm a German strongpoint under cover of a smoke screen

12. An effective shower except that most of the water was supposed to be saved by the lower tin!

13. After days of action with only water to drink, this Australian takes a long pull at a bottle of beer

14. Sherman tanks advance to the front, 5 November 1942

15. General Montgomery standing in front of his General Grant tank (Monty). This tank took the General from Alamein to the River Sangro

16. A Sherman tank leaves landing craft in the Sicily landings

17. This fuel dump near Cesaro gives some idea of the vast amount of materials which were transported to Sicily to support the Allied invasion

18. This Italian coastal gun-battery was part of the enemy defences which were deployed along parts of the Sicilian coast to prevent further Allied landings while the enemy troops withdrew to the mainland

19. Highlanders unload parcels of cigarettes sent as a present from General Montgomery to the men of the Eighth Army

ACKNOWLEDGEMENTS

The publishers wish to thank the following for permission to reproduce the copyright illustrations: The Keystone Press Agency Limited, numbers 16, 17, 18, and 19 in Book One, The Imperial War Museum for all others.

The publishers also wish to express their special thanks to Mr C. D. Hamilton for his invaluable help and advice.

EL ALAMEIN TO THE RIVER SANGRO

FOREWORD

I am anxious to place on record an authoritative and factual account of the activities of the Eighth Army during the period that I commanded the Army. This period was from 13 August 1942 to 31 December 1943; during which time the Army advanced from Alamein to the Sangro River (in Italy). This book contains the story of those days and I have based it on my personal diary.

The Eighth Army was a very happy family. It went from Alamein to half way up Italy without losing a battle or even a serious action, and without ever withdrawing a yard. As a result it acquired a very high morale; the men had confidence in themselves and in their leaders; they knew they were fine soldiers and they looked it: every man an emperor. It was a wonderful experience to command such an Army in the days of its greatest successes.

Montgomery of Alamein
Field-Marshal.

3

THE ADVANCE OF THE EIGHTH ARMY
FROM
EL ALAMEIN TO THE RIVER SANGRO
23rd Oct 1942–31st Dec 1943.

Scale 1/12,000,000
1 Inch = 189.39 Miles

MILES
100 50 0 100 200 300 400

ITALY
RIVER SANGRO
NAPLES
TARANTO
PALERMO
SICILY
CATANIA
MALTA
MARETH
TUNIS
TUNISIA
TRIPOLI
TRIPOLITANIA
BENGHAZI
CYRENAICA
TOBRUK
ALEXANDRIA
EL ALAMEIN
EGYPT

INTRODUCTION

This book tells the story of the Eighth Army's operations in the Mediterranean from El Alamein, 13 August 1942, to the crossing of the River Sangro in Italy, and subsequent operations there until 31 December 1943.

The story concerns primarily the military aspect of the Eighth Army's operations during this period, but the part played by the Royal Navy, and the Royal Air Force in the campaigns in Africa, Sicily, and Italy will not be forgotten.

At all times the Eighth Army was operating with one of its flanks on the sea coast. This fact enabled the Royal Navy to participate in many of our battles and actions, and units of the Fleet were always at hand giving invaluable assistance by bombardment from the sea. Moreover, the progress of the Army was largely governed by the speed with which it could capture and open up ports upon its way; in this matter the Royal Navy played a vital part in assisting our advance. The technique of opening up a port which had been heavily bombed from the air and later deliberately demolished by the enemy in his withdrawal, was developed to a remarkable degree. It has been shown that whatever skill the enemy may employ in his endeavours to prevent the use of a captured port, it can quickly be got working again, and in a short time can be supplying the immense needs of the ground troops and air forces which depend upon it.

A tribute, too, must be paid to the officers and men of the Merchant Navy whose ships brought the material of war from our base to the forward ports. The part they played in our victories was unspectacular; it was nevertheless vital and was accomplished with great heroism and bravery.

The part played by the Royal Air Force in these campaigns was truly tremendous. Mention is constantly made in this story of its operations with the Eighth Army, but in the briefest outline only. It would be difficult for me to pay an adequate tribute to the work and achievements of the Desert Air Force; suffice it to say here that the Desert Air Force and the Eighth Army formed one close, integrated family: collectively they were one great fighting machine, working with a single purpose, and at all times with a single joint plan.

THE CAMPAIGN IN NORTH AFRICA FROM EL ALAMEIN, 13 AUGUST 1942, TO THE END IN TUNISIA, 12 MAY 1943

CHAPTER ONE

THE SITUATION IN THE EIGHTH ARMY IN AUGUST 1942

At the close of the Axis summer offensive, the battle front in the Western Desert was finally stabilized on a line running approximately north and south from the sea at Tel el Eisa to Qaret el Himeimat: a 35-mile front about 60 miles west of Alexandria.

The Eighth Army defensive positions, known as the El Alamein Line, were constructed astride the gap between the sea and the Qattara Depression, blocking the gateway to the Nile Delta. The original line had been laid out in 1941.

Facing our defences the Axis forces, nominally under Italian command but in fact controlled by Field-Marshal Erwin Rommel, comprised five equivalent German divisions and nine Italian divisions. The German Panzer Army Africa included the German Africa Corps (15 and 21 Panzer Divisions), 90 Light and 164 Infantry Divisions, and the Ramcke brigade of parachutists. The Italians were organized in three corps (10, 20, and 21) and included two armoured divisions—Ariete and Littorio.

The Eighth Army front was held by 13 and 30 Corps. The Army disposed six divisions and certain independent armoured and infantry brigades. It was an Imperial force in the truest sense, for it included 9 Australian Division, 5 (later replaced by 4) Indian Division, 2 New Zealand Division, 1 South African Division, and 7 Armoured and 50 Infantry Divisions. There were also Greek and French contingents.

The reverses suffered during the summer of 1942 had left the Eighth Army, in the words of Mr Churchill, 'brave but baffled'. The troops knew that they were worthy of greater

9

things, and indeed the divisions comprised some very fine fighting material. But they had had lost confidence in their higher leadership, they lacked a sound battle technique, and they were deficient of equipment and weapons comparable to those of the Germans. It was clear that Rommel was preparing further attacks, and the morale and determination of our troops was undermined by plans for further withdrawals. The 'atmosphere' was wrong.

Such were my impressions when I arrived in the Western Desert and assumed command of the Eighth Army on 13 August 1942.

My mandate was to destroy the Axis forces in North Africa, and it was immediately apparent that the first step necessary was the initiation of a period of reorganization, re-equipment, and training. While this was being done, I would have to defeat any attempt by the enemy to break through the Alamein defences, and ensure a firm front behind which a striking force could be prepared for the offensive. On my journey from England, I had decided that the Eighth Army required a reserve corps, well equipped and highly trained. This corps (consisting primarily of armoured divisions) would be trained as the spearhead in our offensives, and would never be used to hold static fronts. The Germans had a reserve formation of this kind—the German Africa Corps—based on two crack Panzer divisions. Our lack of a similar formation in the past had meant that we had never been properly balanced. 'Balance' on the battlefield implies the disposal of available forces in such a way that it is never necessary to react to the enemy's thrusts and moves; a balanced army proceeds relentlessly with its plans in spite of what the enemy may do.

I decided, therefore, that the formation, equipping, and training of a reserve corps, strong in armour, must begin at once: as a matter of priority.

THE NEW DEFENSIVE POLICY AT ALAMEIN

My immediate concern was to ensure that the Alamein

Line was securely held. Realizing that the Army might have to withstand a renewed Axis offensive in the immediate future, I ordered at once a new defensive policy.

All existing instructions and plans for further withdrawals were cancelled, and I made it clear that there would be no withdrawal from the Alamein Line; if Rommel attacked, we would fight him where we stood. This change of policy necessitated major alterations in our defences, in particular to give them additional depth, and stocks of ammunition, water, and rations had to be increased in the forward areas. These matters were rapidly put in hand. My initial tour of the battle zone convinced me of the vital importance of the Alam Halfa ridge, which I found virtually undefended. It will be seen from the map that this ridge was several miles in the rear of the Alamein Line; it commanded a wide area of desert country, and was essentially one of the keys to the whole defensive system. If the enemy penetrated the Alamein defences in the southern sectors, his subsequent progress would depend on securing this ridge. If it remained in our hands, it would serve either as a base from which to block the enemy's progress to the north towards Ruweisat ridge (the backbone of our defences in the central sector) or alternatively to cut the axis of any hostile thrust attempting to strike east or north-east towards the Nile. I considered a whole division was required to garrison this ridge as a lay-back position, and asked at once for 44 Division to be sent up to me from the Delta, where it had recently arrived from England.

I ordered that divisions should be concentrated and fought as such; this ended the employment of brigade groups, Jock Columns, and the tactical methods which caused divisions to be split up, but to which recourse had been made in the past because of shortage of troops. As part of this policy, I made it clear that armour and artillery develop their maximum effectiveness when employed in mass, and instructions to implement their use in this way were issued.

11

When I took over command, the Army and Air Headquarters were widely separated, and lacked that close personal relationship which is so essential. I therefore moved my Headquarters to a site adjacent to Air Headquarters, where commanders and staffs could plan and work together as one team.

Lastly, I found a number of higher commanders were tired and in great need of a rest, and I initiated certain changes in order to bring fresh minds to bear on the problem in front of us.

Having established a firm defensive policy, I turned to detailed consideration of the reorganization of the Army, and the formation of the reserve corps—which was to be 10 Corps. During the last weeks of August preparations to this end began to take shape. The reaction within the Eighth Army to the measures I have described was most enthusiastic. The morale of the troops was in the ascendant and their confidence was becoming re-established.

This was the situation when, towards the end of August, it became clear that Rommel intended to attack during the coming full moon.

CHAPTER TWO

THE BATTLE OF ALAM HALFA,
31 AUGUST 1942

On 29 August Rommel announced to his troops that in two or three days they would be in Alexandria, and issued a special order of the day in which he proclaimed that the forthcoming attack would accomplish the 'final annihilation of the enemy'.

His attacks began just after midnight 30/31 August with three simultaneous thrusts. The most northerly attempt was easily repulsed by the Australians and was no more than a raid. In the centre a heavier holding attack, which had lost direction, hit the right of 5 Indian Division, and achieved some initial success. The enemy was ejected from the Ruweisat ridge only after a strong counter attack had been put in at first light on 31 August.

The main thrust was made in the south: between the left flank of the New Zealand Division and Himeimat. Here Rommel employed both 15 and 21 Panzer Divisions, 90 Light Division, and 20 Italian Corps which included Ariete and Littorio Armoured Divisions. By 1000 hours 31 August strong tank columns had penetrated our minefields and were moving eastwards between Gaballa and the Ragil Depression. Further north 90 Light Division had some difficulty in crossing the minefields and did not reach Deir el Muhafid until the evening; between the German wings three Italian divisions were operating but, of these, during the whole engagement the Trieste Division alone succeeded in penetrating the mine belts. Our mobile troops of 7 Armoured Division watching the southern flank were forced back in face of this onslaught and, in accordance with their orders, avoided becoming pinned to the ground. 4 Light

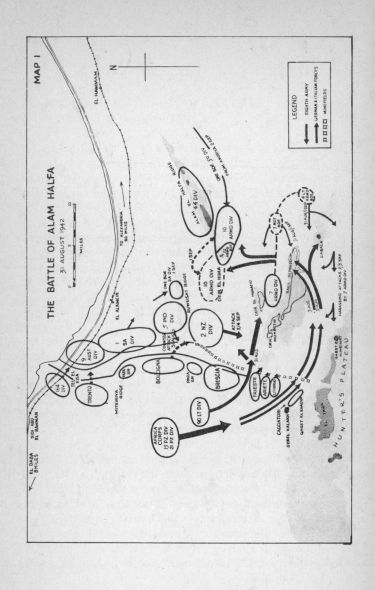

MAP I

THE BATTLE OF ALAM HALFA
31 AUGUST 1942

LEGEND
EIGHTH ARMY
GERMAN & ITALIAN FORCES
MINEFIELDS

Armoured Brigade withdrew on Gaballa, and from that area mounted harassing attacks against the flank of the enemy penetration. Further north, 7 Motor Brigade was similarly employed.

My main preoccupation during 31 August was to determine exactly the direction of the enemy thrust line. I hoped that he would move in a tight wheel to the north towards Alam Halfa, and not wide towards El Hammam. Our deception measures had been directed towards that end. During the late afternoon, the enemy armour began to move northeast, in fact directly towards the area for which the Eighth Army layout was designed. A strong wind was blowing and the Royal Air Force was unable to hinder the advance owing to the dust. By about 1700 hours enemy tanks made contact with 22 Armoured Brigade which was in position to the south of the Alam Halfa ridge. 22 Armoured Brigade met this attack on ground of its own choosing, and the enemy was driven off with heavy casualties.

Towards dusk, dust conditions improved and the night bombers took off. Enemy concentrations were pounded throughout the night, and this began a period of intense day and night air action which was a very important factor in our success.

By the morning of 1 September it was clear to me that the enemy axis of advance was directed on the Alam Halfa ridge and thence northwards to the Ruweisat ridge. He was attempting to roll up our line: working from south to north.

Until I was sure of the direction of the main enemy thrust, I had concentrated the bulk of the armour, under Headquarters 10 Armoured Division, to the south of Alam Halfa, where it blocked any attempt to strike north-east and east in order to by-pass our positions and make straight for the Delta. Having established the enemy's intention I was able to switch the armour to the area between the Alam Halfa ridge, held by 44 Division, and the New Zealand positions in the Alamein Line proper. The ground had been reconnoitred in detail by 10 Armoured Division, and when

15

Rommel renewed his attacks northwards I would be well disposed to inflict heavy losses on his Panzer formations. By the middle of the day, I had nearly 400 tanks in the vital area. At the same time Ruweisat ridge was strengthened by the addition of one brigade, which I withdrew from the front of the South African Division. In order to preserve balance, I brought forward a brigade of 50 Division from Amiriya to the area vacated by 10 Armoured Division south of the Alam Halfa feature.

I was now confident of holding the enemy's attacks, and of preventing infiltration behind the main defensive position. I began to consider regrouping: in order to form reserves and to seize the initiative.

During the morning of 1 September, the enemy had renewed his attacks against 22 Armoured Brigade in position. He achieved nothing and, having again suffered considerable casualties, drew off to the south. He returned to the charge during the afternoon: but the whole of 10 Armoured Division was now firmly established in its new positions, and once more the Panzer formations disengaged with heavy losses.

The relentless pounding of enemy concentrations from the air continued throughout the day.

During the afternoon, I ordered planning to begin for a counter stroke which would give us the initiative. I decided to thin out in 30 Corps sector in the north so as to provide reserves, and to order 13 Corps to prepare to close the gap in our minefields through which the enemy attack had come. The operation would be developed southwards from the New Zealand sector, and proceed methodically and by easy stages.

On 2 September the Axis forces proved reluctant to resume the offensive. They were plainly disconcerted by their failure to draw our armour from its prepared positions. No doubt, too, they were finding the administrative situation difficult. 7 Armoured Division had a good day and intensified its harassing operations north and west of Himeimat, while the Desert Air Force continued to cause great damage and confusion to the enemy.

After visiting the Corps Headquarters, I decided that 13 Corps operations to close the minefield gaps would begin on the night 3/4 September. New Zealand Division would be reinforced for the task by two British infantry brigades. Should the enemy show signs of pulling out, all formations would close in and employ 'jabbing' tactics. I emphasized the importance of destroying soft-skinned vehicles; the more supply lorries we could knock out the greater would be the strain on Rommel's administration. The enemy was known to be short of petrol, and a costly but most effective night bomber raid on Tobruk harbour had done much to aggravate the position. Moreover we had made careful plans to ensure that none of our fuel or supplies fell into his hands.

First light reports on 3 September indicated that the enemy had withdrawn from contact and moved south. His main forces seemed to have edged slightly westwards, leaving the area they vacated strewn with derelict vehicles. I issued very precise instructions at this stage, since it was important to resist any temptation to rush into the attack. The standard of training of the Eighth Army formations was such that I was not prepared to loose them headlong into the enemy; moreover my purpose was to restore the line, and to proceed methodically with my own preparations for the big offensive later on. I therefore ordered that there would be no movement westwards from our main fortified positions in the Alamein Line except by patrols and light forces, and that the attacks to close the gap were to proceed vigorously: but methodically and under careful control. The harassing attacks, particularly those directed against enemy mechanical transport, were to continue with the utmost intensity.

On the afternoon of 3 September three large enemy columns were moving west from the minefield area. The operations of 7 Armoured Division on their southern flank were strengthened and the weight of our air attacks was stepped up to its maximum. On the night 3/4 September the

New Zealand Division began to attack southwards as the first stage to closing the gap in the minefields. The reaction was fierce. Bitter fighting took place, and the enemy launched heavy and repeated counter attacks on 4 September to repel our attempts to bottle him in. We did not succeed in cutting him off, but he was forced slowly and relentlessly back throughout 4 and 5 September. At dawn on the following day fighting continued between our two minefield belts, and it was clear that he meant to retain possession of this area and was prepared to fight for it.

At 0700 hours on 7 September I decided to call off the battle, and to leave the enemy in possession of the western edge of our original minefields, organizing fresh positions for the Eighth Army on the eastern edge of them. There were definite advantages in keeping some additional enemy strength on my southern flank.

All energies of the Army could now be directed again to the business of building up our striking force and preparing for the decisive blow.

SOME REFLECTIONS ON THE BATTLE OF ALAM HALFA

The Eighth Army fought as an integrated Army under the direct control of Army Headquarters. Artillery and armour were used in concentrations, and had been so positioned that the enemy armoured thrusts were dealt with quickly and effectively on ground of our own choosing. The initial layout of our forces, together with speedy regrouping required by the course of the action, had ensured preservation of balance throughout the battlefield. It had thus been unnecessary to conform to Rommel's thrusts, and in our own time we seized the initiative and completed the defeat of the enemy. The tremendous power of the air arm in close co-operation with the land battle was well demonstrated in the operation; the Army and Air Force worked to a combined plan, made possible because the Army and Air Commanders, and their staffs, were working together at one Headquarters.

The victory at Alam Halfa had a profound effect on the

Eighth Army. The morale of the soldiers became outstanding. Rommel had been defeated in his purpose, and had suffered severe casualties. The confidence of the troops in the higher command was re-established, and they entered into the preparations for the decisive battle that was to come with tremendous enthusiasm.

I think that this battle has never received the interest or attention it deserves. It was a vital action, because had we lost it, we might well have lost Egypt. In winning it we paved the way for success at El Alamein and the subsequent advance to Tunisia.

An interesting feature of the story of operations against the Germans in North Africa is the recurrence of similar circumstances before the Battle of Mareth, later in the campaign. There, also, success in a defensive battle at Medenine on 6 March paved the way for decisive victory in our subsequent offensive at Mareth on 20 March.

CHAPTER THREE

PREPARATIONS FOR THE BATTLE OF EL ALAMEIN

The Battle of Alam Halfa had interfered with our preparations for the formation of a reserve corps, and had caused us some delay. As soon as the situation had been restored, however, no time was lost in continuing with our plans.

10 Corps (General Lumsden) was to consist of 1 Armoured Division, 10 Armoured Division (including two armoured brigades), and 2 New Zealand Division (with an armoured brigade under command). This Corps was concentrated for training and re-equipment in the rear areas. 2 New Zealand Division was relieved in the line by 44 Division, whose positions at Alam Halfa were taken over by 51 Division, recently arrived from the United Kingdom.

My policy at this stage was to build up the Army on three basic fundamentals: leadership, equipment, and training. By early October I was satisfied with the leadership aspect; my subordinate commanders were sound, and I had every confidence in them.

The equipment situation improved rapidly. Sherman tanks, sent to us at the personal instigation of President Roosevelt, started arriving in the Delta from America in August, and were issued to 10 Corps. In the Sherman we had at last a match for the German tanks. We had moreover a great weight of artillery and there was plenty of ammunition.

My great anxiety was that the state of training was still not good, and it was becoming clear that I would have to be very careful to ensure that units and formations were not given tasks which would be beyond their capabilities. I would have to stage-manage the forthcoming battle in such a way that the troops would be able to do what was demanded of them, and I must not be too ambitious in my demands.

During this period of preparation, I was working out the plan for the Battle of Alamein. It was because of shortcomings in the standard of training in the Army, that I had to alter, early in October, the whole conception of how I intended to fight the battle.

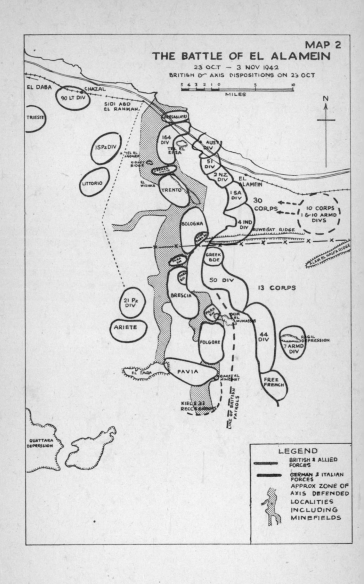

MAP 2

THE BATTLE OF EL ALAMEIN

23 OCT — 3 NOV 1942

BRITISH & AXIS DISPOSITIONS ON 23 OCT

5 4 3 2 1 0   5   10

MILES

N

EL DABA   CHAZAL

90 LT DIV

TRIESTE   SIDI ABD EL RAHMAN

URESAGUERI

15 PZ DIV   164 DIV   AUST DIV

TEL EL EISA

51 DIV

TEL EL AQQAQIR   2 NZ DIV   EL ALAMEIN

KIDNEY RIDGE

LITTORIO   1 SA DIV

EL WISHKA   30 CORPS   10 CORPS & 10 ARMD DIVS

TRENTO

4 IND DIV

BOLOGNA   RUWEISAT RIDGE

ALAM EL HALFA RIDGE

GREEK BDE

50 DIV   13 CORPS

21 PZ DIV   BRESCIA

RAGIL DEPRESSION

ARIETE   DEIR EL MUNASSIB   44 DIV   7 ARMD DIV

FOLGORE

EL TAQA   PAVIA   FREE FRENCH

QARET EL HIMEIMAT

KIEL & 33 RECCE GROUP   LINE OF BRITISH PATROLS

QUATTARA DEPRESSION

LEGEND

————— BRITISH & ALLIED FORCES

▬▬▬▬▬ GERMAN & ITALIAN FORCES

APPROX ZONE OF AXIS DEFENDED LOCALITIES INCLUDING MINEFIELDS

THE BATTLE OF EL ALAMEIN, 23 OCTOBER 1942

MAJOR CONSIDERATIONS AFFECTING THE PLAN

Full moon was on 24 October. A full moon was essential for the operation, since there was no open flank, and we had to make gaps in the minefields and to blow a hole through the enemy's defensive system during the night. The earliest therefore that we could mount the offensive was on the night 23/24 October.

The enemy had made good use of the lull after his abortive attack to strengthen and deepen his defences. In the northern sector he had three belts of defended localities and minefields and any attack by us was intended to lose both force and direction within this system itself. In the south, the defences were not so highly organized, but were sited to canalize any penetration we might make. In general the minefields alone extended for some 5,000 to 9,000 yards in depth. The enemy positions were held by one German and five Italian divisions, together with a German parachute brigade; detached German infantry elements were used to stiffen the Italian sectors. In reserve in the north were the 15 Panzer and Italian Littorio Armoured Divisions, and further to the rear, on the coast, was 90 Light Division. In reserve in the south there were 21 Panzer and the Ariete Armoured Divisions. On the Egyptian frontier stood the Pistoia Division.

It was extremely difficult to achieve any form of surprise. It seemed impossible to conceal from the enemy that we meant to launch an attack. At best we could deceive him about the direction of our main thrusts and the date by which we would be ready to begin.

In planning the Battle of Alamein the main difficulties confronting us were three: first, the problem of blowing a hole in the enemy positions; secondly, the despatch of a Corps strong in armour through the hole into enemy territory; and lastly, the development of operations so as to destroy the Axis forces.

In September I had been working on the idea of attacking the enemy simultaneously on both flanks—the main attack being made in the north by 30 Corps (General Leese). This operation would force a gap across the enemy's defensive system through which 10 Corps would pass. 10 Corps would position itself on ground of its own choosing *astride the enemy supply routes*; the enemy armour would deploy against it, and be destroyed: probably piecemeal, as I hoped to keep it dispersed as long as possible. The attack of 13 Corps (General Horrocks) in the south would draw off enemy armour to that flank, and thus weaken at least the initial opposition to 10 Corps.

As I have mentioned already, early in October I changed the conception of how I would fight the battle, because I was not satisfied that we were capable of achieving success in a plan so ambitious.

It had been generally accepted that the plan in a modern battle should aim first at destroying the enemy's armour, and that once this had been accomplished, the unarmoured portion of his army would be dealt with readily. I decided to reverse this concept and to destroy first the unarmoured formations. While doing this I would hold off the armoured divisions, which would be tackled subsequently. In broad terms, the fighting elements of Rommel's army comprised holding troops (mostly unarmoured) who manned defences and guarded essential areas of ground; and mobile troops (mostly armoured) whose role was offensive. The mobile troops were used to deliver counter attacks during defensive periods, and to form the spearhead of advance in the offensive. If the holding troops could be destroyed, the enemy

24

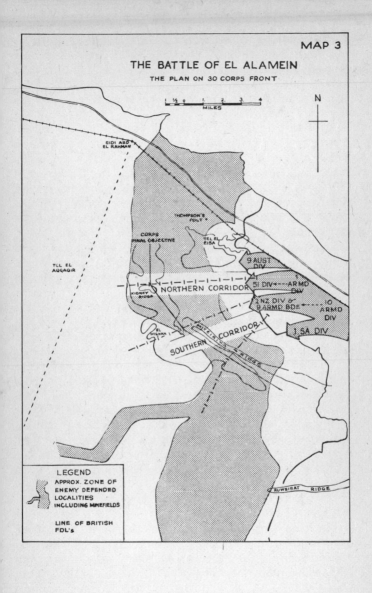

MAP 3

THE BATTLE OF EL ALAMEIN

THE PLAN ON 30 CORPS FRONT

1 ½ 0   1   2   3   4
MILES

N

SIDI ABD
EL RAHMAN

THOMPSON'S
POST

TEL EL
EISA

CORPS
FINAL OBJECTIVE

TLL EL
AQQAQIR

9 AUST
DIV

KIDNEY
RIDGE

NORTHERN CORRIDOR

51 DIV — ARMD
DIV

EL
WISHKA

2 NZ DIV &
9 ARMD BDE

10
ARMD
DIV

MITEIRIYA RIDGE

SOUTHERN CORRIDOR

1 SA DIV

RUWEISAT RIDGE

LEGEND
APPROX. ZONE OF
ENEMY DEFENDED
LOCALITIES
INCLUDING MINEFIELDS

LINE OF BRITISH
FDL's

would be unable to secure ground vital to the action of his armoured forces; these would be denied firm bases from which to manoeuvre and within which to refurbish, and their supply routes would lie open to interruption. In these circumstances the armoured forces would be forced to withdraw or perish.

My idea therefore was to aim first at the methodical destruction of the infantry divisions holding the enemy's defensive system. This would be accomplished by means of a 'crumbling' process, carefully organized from a series of firm bases: an operation within the capabilities of my troops. For success, the method depended on holding off the enemy's armour while the 'crumbling' manoeuvre was carried out. It was also vital that the 'break-in' battle, designed to gain a foothold in the enemy's defences, should achieve complete success, so that the enemy infantry might be attacked from the flank and rear and its supply routes in the forward area could be cut.

The enemy's armour would obviously not sit still and watch the gradual destruction of the infantry; it would be launched into counter attacks. If I could position my armour beyond the area of the 'crumbling' operations, on ground of its own choosing, the enemy tanks would have to attack in conditions favourable to us, and could be held off. The minefields, particularly those west of the main Axis positions, would restrict the approaches available to those enemy tanks which might try to counter attack our assaulting units while they were dealing with the defending infantry. If the approaches themselves were closed by our own tanks in position, we would be able to proceed relentlessly with our plans.

My orders for the battle, issued on 6 October, provided for three simultaneous attacks.

The main thrust by 30 Corps in the north was to be made on a front of four divisions, with the task of forcing two corridors through the enemy's minefields. 10 Corps was to pass through these corridors.

26

In the south, 13 Corps was to mount two operations: one into the area east of Gebel Kalakh and Qaret el Khadim, the other further south directed on Himeimat and the Taqa feature.

13 and 30 Corps having broken into the enemy's defences were to undertake the methodical destruction of the troops holding the forward positions.

10 Corps had as its ultimate task the destruction of the enemy armour, and was to be manoeuvred so as to prevent enemy interference with 30 Corps operations; it would assist, as opportunity offered, in the 'crumbling' process.

The role of 13 Corps was primarily to mislead the enemy into believing that our main thrust was being delivered in the south, and to contain enemy forces there: particularly 21 Panzer Division. 7 Armoured Division was available for the operation, but I ordered that it was to be kept intact on the southern flank, in order to preserve balanced dispositions throughout the front. Whereas everything was to be ready to pass this formation through the minefields and to exploit it in a swing northwards towards Daba, I made it clear that the attack was not to be pressed if heavy casualties were likely to result.

My orders emphasized that it was vital to retain the initiative and to keep up sustained pressure on the enemy. The troops were to take advantage of any weakening and were to avoid any long pauses which might give the enemy time to recover his balance.

The break-in operation was to be facilitated by a very heavy counter-battery plan, the effect of which was to be strengthened by switching the whole of the bomber effort on to the artillery areas as soon as the battle began. I realized that following the break-in, a real dog-fight would ensue. I was confident that our resources were sufficient to withstand the strain which this would impose. The essentials of the battle would be the retention of the initiative, the maintenance of pressure on the enemy, and the preservation of balance so that it would be unnecessary to react to the enemy's thrusts.

The Royal Air Force plan of operations began with the winning of the air battle before the attack opened. Having obtained ascendancy over the German Air Force, the whole of the air effort was to be available to co-operate intimately in the land battle.

The cover plan for the battle was worked out in August and September. It aimed at misleading the enemy about the direction of the main thrusts and the date of our readiness for the attack.

The basis of 'visual deception' was the preservation of a constant density of vehicles throughout the zone of operations, so that the enemy would be denied the inferences made from the changes disclosed in day-to-day air photographs. By means of pooled transport resources (enlarged by the reduction of divisional holdings) and by the construction of large numbers of dummy lorries, the layout and density of vehicles required for the assault in the northern sector was established on the ground as early as 1 October. During the period of forward concentration of 51 and 2 New Zealand Divisions and 10 Corps, the substitute transport was replaced at night by the operational transport of the divisions concerned. Guns, limbers, and squads of reinforcing artillery units were dealt with in a similar way. The rear areas whence these units and formations came were maintained at their full vehicle quota by the erection of dummies as the real transport moved out. Dumps were concealed by elaborate camouflage and by stacking stores to resemble vehicles. A month before the attack, slit trenches were dug, in which (when the time came) the assaulting infantry could be concealed.

Meanwhile active measures were employed to cause the enemy to believe the main blow would be delivered in the south. A dummy pipeline was started late in September, and progress in the work was timed to indicate its completion by the first week in November; dummy dumps were also made working to a similar date. Headquarters 8 Armoured Division was used to assist, with its wireless network, the notion that armoured forces were moving to the southern flank.

An essential feature of my plan was that every commander in the Army, down to the rank of Lieutenant-Colonel, should know from me personally how I proposed to fight the battle, what issues depended on it, and what were the main difficulties we were likely to encounter. I toured the Army addressing the officers.

On 21 and 22 October, the battle was explained to the troops by their officers.

I was determined that the soldiers should go into battle having been worked up into a great state of enthusiasm, and realizing fully what was expected of them.

Heavy and sustained air attacks against the Axis air forces and land communications reached a crescendo on 22 October. The degree of air superiority thus achieved was such that throughout 23 October our aircraft maintained continuous fighter patrols over enemy landing grounds without interference.

Concentration in the forward assembly areas was completed during the night 22/23 October, and by first light, all formations were dug in and camouflaged. The assaulting infantry spent the day of 23 October unobserved in the slits dug in front of our foremost positions, and it was clear from the absence of shelling of our positions that we would indeed achieve tactical surprise.

The stage was set. During the morning my personal message was read out to all ranks:

> 'The Battle which is now about to begin will be
> one of the decisive battles of history.
> It will be the turning point of the war . . .
> The Lord mighty in battle will give us the victory.'

With these words the Eighth Army was launched into battle.

23–24 October 1942

Operations 23/24 October

The night of 23 October was still and clear. At 2140 hours, in the bright moonlight, the Eighth Army artillery opened on located enemy batteries. Over a thousand field and medium guns were employed, and the effect was terrific.

At 2200 hours fire was switched to the enemy's foremost positions, and the assaulting divisions of 13 and 30 Corps advanced to the attack.

In the north, the four divisions of 30 Corps attacked in line. 9 Australian and 51 Divisions, responsible for forcing the northern corridor through the minefields, attacked west from their positions just north of Miteiriya ridge; the New Zealanders and South Africans thrust in a south-south-westerly direction on to the ridge itself, and were to establish the southern corridor. At the same time 4 Indian Division carried out a strong raid against enemy positions on the western end of Ruweisat ridge, and in the extreme north an Australian brigade made a feint attack between Tel el Eisa and the sea.

Heavy fighting continued all night against stiffening resistance, but by 0530 hours most of the final objectives had been reached. The two corridors had been pushed through the main minefield belts and supporting weapons of the infantry were moving forward. 9 Armoured Brigade (2 New Zealand Division) was also reported to be progressing well through the southern corridor.

Behind the divisions of 30 Corps, 1 and 10 Armoured Divisions of 10 Corps crossed their start line at 0200 hours and made for the northern and southern routes respectively. Both formations however got behind schedule. 1 Armoured Division was delayed because a strong enemy locality held up 51 Division. When 10 Armoured Division came up to the Miteiriya ridge, enemy artillery and anti-tank gun fire prohibited its progress. 9 Armoured Brigade of 2 New

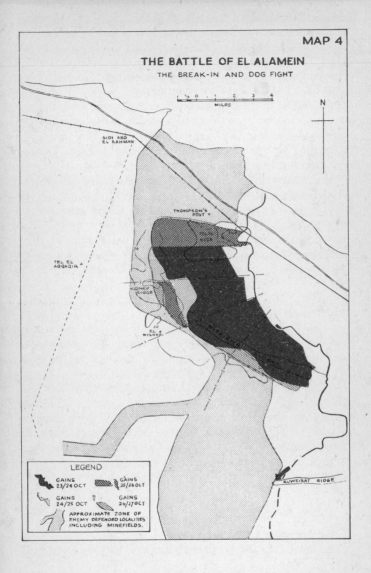

MAP 4

THE BATTLE OF EL ALAMEIN
THE BREAK-IN AND DOG FIGHT

MILES

N

SIDI ABD
EL RAHMAN

THOMPSON'S
POST

TEL EL
AQQAQIR

KIDNEY
RIDGE

EL
WISHKA

MITEIRIYA RIDGE

RUWEISAT RIDGE

LEGEND

GAINS
23/24 OCT

GAINS
25/26 OCT

GAINS
24/25 OCT

GAINS
26/27 OCT

APPROXIMATE ZONE OF
ENEMY DEFENDED LOCALITIES
INCLUDING MINEFIELDS.

Zealand Division got forward of the ridge, but met further minefields and also heavy anti-tank gun fire. The armour remained behind the Miteiriya feature and engaged the enemy at long range. 15 Panzer Division delivered a series of minor counter attacks which were beaten off with considerable casualties to the enemy tanks.

Meanwhile in 13 Corps sector to the south, an operation was mounted by 7 Armoured and 44 Divisions with the object of forcing two gaps in the minefields north of Himeimat. At the same time 1 Fighting French Brigade attacked Hunter's Plateau.

The attempt to breach the western field failed after being hung up by scattered mines between the two major belts. 13 Corps therefore resorted to 'crumbling' action between the belts during 24 October and achieved valuable results. The French took their objective, but soft sand delayed their supporting weapons, and they were driven back by a counter attack delivered by the Kiel Group—a German armoured column.

Situation on 24 October

In the north we had successfully broken into the enemy positions and secured a good bridgehead. But attempts to pass the armour into the open and to the west of the Axis defensive system had been unsuccessful.

My plan was now to force 1 and 10 Armoured Divisions into the open as quickly as possible, and to commence 'crumbling' operations to the south-west by 2 New Zealand Division. I also ordered a strong raid westwards from the Ruweisat ridge by 30 Corps and completion of the gaps through the southern minefield by 13 Corps.

THE 'DOG-FIGHT'

24—30 October 1942

Operations 24/25 October

The attack on the north corridor axis was resumed by 1

Armoured Division and 51 Division at 1500 hours on 24 October. My orders were very firm and produced good results; by 1800 hours 2 Armoured Brigade (1 Armoured Division) had broken out from the western minefield, and was taking up positions beyond.

On the southern corridor axis, 10 Armoured Division supported by 30 Corps artillery, renewed its attack at 2200 hours. During the night reports showed that the operation was not making progress. I feared that my plan for getting this formation through the mine belt was in danger of failure and at 0400 hours, 25 October, I issued orders that it must and would get forward. By 0800 hours, the leading armoured brigade was reported in position, 2,000 yards west of the minefield area, and in touch with 1 Armoured Division on its right. The leading regiment of the other armoured brigade of the division had also cleared the enemy's main position.

Meanwhile 9 Armoured Brigade of 2 New Zealand Division was clear of the corridor, and was operating south-west according to plan.

During 25 October, 15 Panzer Division again made a series of counter attacks, including one near Kidney Ridge in which about 100 tanks were used. Our armour was now in position, and repulsed these attacks with heavy casualties to the enemy.

In the 13 Corps area, 44 Division renewed its efforts to gap the minefields during the night 24/25 October and was successful. A small bridgehead was formed and 4 Light Armoured Brigade was passed through. Scattered mines and an anti-tank gun screen were encountered however, and it was apparent that heavy casualties would be sustained if the attack were pressed home. On the morning of 25 October, I authorized 13 Corps to break off this action, in accordance with my policy of maintaining 7 Armoured Division at effective fighting strength. It was essential to maintain the balance of the Army, and as long as 21 Panzer Division was in the south, I required an armoured division in 13 Corps:

and its presence there assisted materially in keeping enemy armour in the south.

On 25 October, 50 Division mounted an attack in the Munassib area. This was not pressed and soon petered out in face of thick wire and anti-personnel mines.

Situation on 25 October

We had now thrust our armour out into positions where it was well placed to meet the enemy tanks and inflict on them heavy casualties. It could function as I had intended, and as long as the enemy attacked us, particularly in isolated and piecemeal fashion, I was well content.

In the south 13 Corps was maintaining the threat well.

My major consideration was now the 'crumbling' process of wearing down the enemy's infantry in the north. It became clear that 2 New Zealand Division's move south-west would be a most costly undertaking, and at midday on 25 October I decided to abandon it and to switch the main 'crumbling' action to the Australian sector. I gave orders for 9 Australian Division to attack north towards the sea, with the object of destroying the German forces in the coastal salient which had been created by our break-in battle. In conjunction with this attack, I provided for operations to be developed westwards by 1 Armoured Division from its position in the bridgehead. If 1 Armoured Division could make progress to the west, the opportunity might come to pass its armoured brigade through to the Rahman track; it could then get behind the enemy holding the salient. In the following days I was constantly considering the problem of establishing armour in the Rahman area, since it was the key to the system of enemy supply routes in rear.

In switching the main 'crumbling' process so radically I hoped to gain surprise and to take a heavy toll of the enemy.

Operations night 25/26 and 26 October

The Australian attack on the night 25/26 October was completely successful. The Germans suffered some 300 casualties.

1 Armoured Division, however, failed to make any progress to the west in its operations in the Kidney Ridge sector.

On 26 October, 1 South African Division and 2 New Zealand Division advanced about 1,000 yards, thus gaining more depth in front of the Miteiriya ridge. The same night, 7 Motor Brigade established itself on Kidney Ridge.

Situation 26 October

I spent the day in detailed consideration of the situation, and it was from this date onwards that plans were evolved culminating in the final break-out operation which was launched on the night 1/2 November.

My tank state showed over 800 runners, and the ammunition situation was sound. But a note of caution was imposed in my planning. The assaulting divisions had suffered considerable casualties, and there was a lack of replacements for the New Zealand and South African Divisions.

The infantry divisions had, according to plan, carried out slow and methodical improvement of their positions by a series of carefully co-ordinated attacks on narrow fronts with limited objectives. In this they had taken heavy toll of the hostile infantry. 30 Corps was now, however, in need of a short pause for reorganization.

The armoured divisions were forward in positions from which heavy casualties had been caused to the enemy armour.

The momentum of the attack, however, was diminishing and 10 Corps had not broken out into open country. The enemy had withdrawn troops and guns from his forward positions in anticipation of our offensive, and we had therefore found him in greater depth than had been expected. Our break-in area was still ringed by a strong anti-tank gun screen, and attempts to pierce it had been unsuccessful.

By evening on 26 October I had decided to regroup, in order to create fresh reserves for further offensive action. The next phase would be in the north again, as I had been impressed with the results of the Australian attack on the night 25/26 October. If I could get behind the enemy holding the coastal salient, I would annihilate or capture a strong force of Germans and perhaps open up the operation along the coastal axis. The first stage of regrouping was the reversion of 2 New Zealand Division into reserve. Its sector was taken over by 1 South African Division, which was relieved in turn by 4 Indian Division. The latter I placed under 13 Corps.

Operations 27 and 28 October

Throughout 27 October the enemy launched heavy armoured counter attacks against Kidney Ridge. These attacks were put in by both 15 and 21 Panzer Divisions, the latter having moved north during the previous night. The enemy was repulsed in all cases, and suffered very heavy losses. 1 Armoured Division alone knocked out nearly fifty German tanks in this engagement.

On 28 October the enemy made a prolonged reconnaissance of Kidney Ridge, probing for soft spots while the two German Panzer Divisions waited in rear. In the evening they began to concentrate for attack, but the Desert Air Force intervened with such effect that the enemy was defeated before he had completed his forming-up.

Situation on 27 and 28 October

On 27 October, I developed my plan for breaking out in the northern sector.

I gave orders for 9 Australian Division to launch a heavy attack northwards on the night 28/29 October.

I intended to destroy the enemy coastal salient, and then drive 30 Corps westwards along the road and railway route to Sidi Abd el Rahman. Holding off the enemy armour, our tanks would operate to the south.

The situation in the south was such that I decided that 13 Corps should become primarily defensive. Every endeavour was to be made by means of patrols and artillery action to

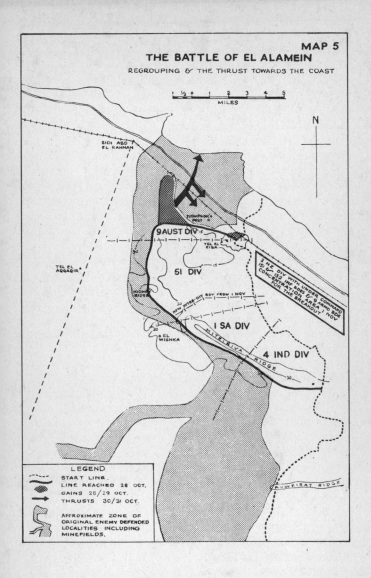

MAP 5

THE BATTLE OF EL ALAMEIN

REGROUPING & THE THRUST TOWARDS THE COAST

MILES

N

SIDI ABD
EL RAHMAN

THOMPSON'S
POST

9 AUST DIV

TEL EL
EISA

TEL EL
AQQAQIR

51 DIV

15

2 NZ DIV WITH UNDER COMMAND
151 & 152 INF BDES & 9 ARMD BDE
CONCENTRATION AREA 1 NOV
FOR THE BREAKOUT

KIDNEY
RIDGE

30

NEW INTER-DIV BDY FROM 1 NOV

20

EL
WISHKA

I SA DIV

MITEIRIYA RIDGE

4 IND DIV

30

RUWEISAT RIDGE

LEGEND

START LINE.
LINE REACHED 28 OCT.
GAINS 28/29 OCT.
THRUSTS 30/31 OCT.

APPROXIMATE ZONE OF
ORIGINAL ENEMY DEFENDED
LOCALITIES INCLUDING
MINEFIELDS.

prolong the enemy's anxiety in this sector, but no further major operations would be staged there. 21 Panzer Division had been contained in the south until the night of 26 October, and our infantry had inflicted heavy casualties on the enemy. 13 Corps had successfully fulfilled its role.

I now ordered the second stage of regrouping. 7 Armoured Division (with a brigade of 44 Division), a brigade of 50 Division, and the Greek Brigade, were to be sent up to the northern sector from 13 Corps; and, to release troops for the forthcoming Australian attack, a brigade of 51 Division relieved 20 Australian Brigade. 1 Armoured Division needed a pause for reorganization, and since it was clear that the whole German Africa Corps was now facing the northern corridor, I turned the sector over to the defensive, and withdrew 1 Armoured Division and 24 Armoured Brigade into reserve.

New Zealand Division was selected to lead the drive westwards, and since it was low in strength, I arranged for the brigades from 13 Corps to be available to work with it and keep it at operational strength.

In this way regrouping of the Army was undertaken, and I was soon to have a strong reserve force ready to stage the break-out and to deliver the knock-out blow.

Operations night 28/29, 29 and 30 October

The Australian attack on night 28/29 October made good progress and about 200 prisoners were taken. A narrow wedge was driven into the enemy's positions, reaching almost to the road between Sidi Abd el Rahman and Tel el Eisa. On the right of the attack very strong opposition and extensive minefields were encountered round Thompson's Post, which was the bastion of the enemy's coastal salient.

During 29 October, and again early on 30 October, repeated counter attacks by tanks and infantry were hurled against the Australians in the wedge, but they held on and retained the ground won.

Situation 29 and 30 October

I learnt during the morning of 29 October that 90 Light Division had moved into the Sidi Abd el Rahman area. This was very significant, for it showed that Rommel was reacting to the threat in the north and had probably guessed my intention of striking west along the road and rail axis.

As a result I modified my plan for the break-out by moving the axis of the westwards drive further to the south, so that the blow would fall mainly on the Italians.

9 Australian Division would resume its threat northwards to the sea on the night 30/31 October. This would prepare the way for the break-out to the west by confirming the enemy's fears in the extreme north. Above all it would probably ensure that 90 Light Division remained about Sidi Abd el Rahman.

On night 31 October/1 November (subsequently postponed 24 hours), 2 New Zealand Division thrusting due west would blow a new gap through the enemy positions just north of the existing northern corridor. Through this gap 10 Corps would pass out into the open desert with 1, 7, and 10 Armoured Divisions and two armoured car regiments. The armoured divisions were to destroy the German Africa Corps and the armoured cars were to operate on the enemy supply routes to intensify the enemy's administrative difficulties—particularly his shortage of petrol. To this operation I gave the name 'Supercharge'.

'Supercharge' was to get us out into the open country and to lead to the disintegration of Rommel's forces in Egypt. We had got to bring the enemy's armour to battle and get astride his lines of communication. 2 New Zealand Division's task involved a penetration of some 6,000 yards on a 4,000 yards front, and I made it clear that should 30 Corps fail to reach its final objectives, *the armoured divisions of 10 Corps were to fight their way through.*

The change of thrust line of 'Supercharge' to the south proved most fortunate. I learnt on 1 November that 21 Panzer Division had joined 90 Light Division in the

Rahman area, so that the road and railway axis was very strongly covered. Rommel was playing into my hands, for the bulk of his German forces was now concentrated on the coast, leaving the Italians to hold the more southerly sectors. I could drive a blow between the Germans and Italians and concentrate on destroying the former.

THE 'BREAK-OUT'

31 October–4 November 1942

Operations 31 October to 3 November

The thrust north started again on the night 30/31 October as planned. The Australians succeeded in crossing the coast road and pushed forward to the sea and then turned eastwards. The Panzer Grenadiers of 164 Division were thus trapped, and the enemy launched a number of furious counter attacks to free them. Towards evening some German tanks from the west succeeded in joining the defenders of Thompson's Post, and eventually the majority of the Germans fought their way out. But the enemy suffered very severe casualties in this action.

At 0100 hours, 2 November, 'Supercharge' began and the assaulting troops advanced behind a creeping barrage.

151 and 152 Infantry Brigades attacked on the main frontage, under command of 2 New Zealand Division. Subsidiary attacks were staged to extend the base of the salient.

9 Armoured Brigade was to pass through the infantry on its final objective and form a bridgehead beyond the track running south from Sidi Abd el Rahman. 1 and 7 Armoured Divisions (and later 10 Armoured Division) were to debouch from this bridgehead, together with the two armoured car regiments detailed for raids deep in the enemy rear.

The operation achieved great success. The new corridor was established and 9 Armoured Brigade reached the Rahman track just before first light. The Royals swung south-west and reached open country, and were followed

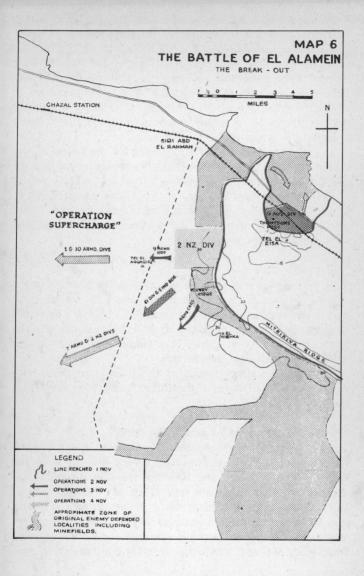

MAP 6

THE BATTLE OF EL ALAMEIN
THE BREAK - OUT

½ 0 1   2   3   4   5
MILES

N

CHAZAL STATION

SIDI ABD
EL RAHMAN

"OPERATION
SUPERCHARGE"

1 & 10 ARMD. DIVS

9 ARMD
BDE

2 NZ DIV
30

TEL EL
AQQAQIR

15 PZ DIV
THOMPSONS
POST

TEL EL
EISA

15

EL DIV & 5 IND BDE

KIDNEY
RIDGE

ARMD CLASH

30

7 ARMD & 2 NZ DIVS

30

EL
WISHKA

MITEIRIYA RIDGE

30

LEGEND

LINE REACHED 1 NOV

OPERATIONS 2 NOV

OPERATIONS 3 NOV

OPERATIONS 4 NOV

APPROXIMATE ZONE OF
ORIGINAL ENEMY DEFENDED
LOCALITIES INCLUDING
MINEFIELDS.

later by 4 South African Armoured Car Regiment which had been considerably delayed in breaking out.

As it became light 9 Armoured Brigade ran into a formidable anti-tank gun screen and during the day suffered over 75 per cent casualties. It hung on tenaciously inflicting losses on the enemy and its action was instrumental in holding the bridgehead. 1 Armoured Division, too, became involved near Tel el Aqqaqir, and a fierce armoured battle ensued in which both sides had losses.

In the afternoon 51 Division extended the salient to the south, and at night 7 Motor Brigade attacked to the west of the Rahman track.

On 3 November, the Desert Air Force reported heavy traffic moving westwards on the coast road, but the enemy anti-tank gun screen held, and 1 Armoured Division was still unable to pierce it.

Situation 3 November

It was now clear that the enemy contemplated a withdrawal, but would have difficulty in getting his troops away owing to shortage of transport and fuel. And so I expected that he would try and hold me off while his evacuation of the Alamein positions proceeded, but I made plans to complete the break-out and get behind him.

I ordered an attack to the south of Tel el Aqqaqir, with the object of outflanking the anti-tank gun screen which was hemming us in.

Operations on night 3/4 and 4 November

On the night 3/4 November 51 Division and a brigade from 4 Indian Division launched a very speedily mounted thrust which reached the Rahman track south of Tel el Aqqaqir on a front of over four miles. My intention was to break through the southern sector of the enemy's anti-tank gun screen which was preventing our penetration; the enemy was not in very great depth in the area and once a gap had been made the way would be clear for our armour to pass out into the open desert, out-flanking the stronger resistance to the north. Very great credit is due to the formations which organized this attack in an extremely short time and carried it through successfully, for by the morning of 4 November the enemy screen had been forced back and reformed facing south-east covering the coast road. The armoured divisions and New Zealanders were set in motion. The Battle of El Alamein had been won. Everywhere the enemy was in full retreat.

THE PURSUIT FROM EL ALAMEIN

I planned to cut off the retreating enemy by swinging north to cut the coast road at the bottlenecks of Fuka and Matruh. 2 New Zealand Division was ordered to Fuka, and 10 Corps to Matruh.

Meanwhile to the south of the break-out area, 13 Corps formed mobile columns which raced westwards to round up the Italians, four of whose divisions had been left by the Germans without transport and with very little food or water.

The Desert Air Force operated at maximum intensity and took every advantage of the exceptional targets which the fleeing enemy presented.

During 4 November 10 Corps encountered the remnants of the enemy armour south of Ghazal. 2 New Zealand Division by-passed these rearguards to the south, but on 5 November had a sharp engagement near Fuka; during the afternoon 4 Light Armoured Brigade broke through the op-position and swung in to the road.

On 5 November I regrouped for the pursuit. 10 Corps (1 and 7 Armoured and 2 New Zealand Divisions) was to lead the chase. 30 Corps I positioned between Matruh and Alamein, and to 13 Corps I assigned the task of clearing up the battlefield.

By nightfall 6 November, advanced troops were nearing the Matruh–Charing Cross where I hoped to cut off a considerable body of the enemy survivors.

Heavy rains interfered with my plans. On 7 November the force was bogged in the desert, with its petrol and supplies held up some miles behind. 1 Armoured Division failed to reach Charing Cross and delay was experienced on the coast in clearing the enemy rearguards at Matruh. The enemy made good use of this respite of some twenty-four hours to retrieve some of his troops and transport, which fled along the coast road, and the long pursuit to the El Agheila position began.

SOME REFLECTIONS ON THE BATTLE OF EL ALAMEIN

The Axis forces in North Africa had sustained a crushing defeat, and indeed only the rain on 6 and 7 November saved them from complete annihilation. Four crack German divisions and eight Italian divisions had ceased to exist as effective fighting formations.

30,000 prisoners, including nine Generals, were taken.

A great number of enemy tanks had been destroyed, and the quantity of guns, transport, aircraft, and stores of all kinds captured or destroyed was immense.

The battle had conformed to the pattern anticipated. The break-in, or battle for position, had given us the tactical advantage; the dog-fight which followed reduced the enemy's strength and resources to a degree which left him unable to withstand the final knock-out blow. The dog-fight demanded rapid re-grouping of forces to create reserves available for switching the axis of operations as the situation required; in this way the initiative was retained, and the battle swung to its desired end.

Tactical surprise was an important factor; the break-in operation achieved it completely, for the enemy had expected our main thrust in the south. In the final thrust again the enemy was deceived; he had prepared for it in the extreme north, and concentrated his German troops to meet it. It was delivered against the Italians, two miles south of the German flank.

The most critical time in the battle was 26 and 27

October. Fighting was intense but the momentum of our attacks was diminishing. It was then that I started drawing divisions into reserve, ready for the final operation. At the time this gave to some the impression that I had decided that we could not break through the enemy and was giving up; but I would say that when you find a commander drawing troops into reserve at a critical moment of the battle, it probably means he is about to win it.

It was always clear in my mind that once a commander defeated his enemy in battle, everything else would be added unto him. The great hazard at El Alamein was whether the enemy would stand and fight it out. He did; he was decisively defeated; the rest was relatively easy. In the previous desert campaigns, Rommel had never been decisively defeated in battle; he had been forced to withdraw, but not because of decisive defeat. There was now a fundamental difference in the problem of the future conduct of the desert war. To this I will refer again, because it was a basic consideration in my plans to ensure that there would never be another Axis recovery and re-entry into Egypt.

CHAPTER FIVE

THE PURSUIT TO THE EL AGHEILA POSITION

There were three major considerations regarding the pursuit after the Battle of El Alamein.

First: the Eighth Army must drive hard to cut off Rommel's remnants; it had been foiled by the rain in the Matruh area, but continued the chase in improving weather on 9 November. The enemy must be given no respite and no opportunity to organize defences to delay us.

Second: there was the importance of establishing the Desert Air Force on forward aerodromes. In conjunction with armoured cars, the Air Force could act as our long range hitting weapon, and greatly increase the confusion of the enemy's withdrawal; at the same time fighter cover could be given to the light forces operating in the van of the pursuit. In the broader picture, it was urgent to establish our Air Forces firmly in Cyrenaica, on airfields from which they could dominate the Central Mediterranean, the Libyan ports and Rommel's long lines of communication along the coast to Benghazi and Tripoli. The immediate object was to operate from the fields in the Egyptian frontier area from which Tobruk could be covered. More important was the Martuba group of airfields, in the Jebel el Akdar, whence the Malta convoys could be safely escorted.

Third: there was the administrative situation. The pace of the pursuit was fast and the strain on administration became increasingly severe. It was essential for us to get the port of Tobruk as quickly as possible and it was also clear that we should have to be prepared to pause at some stage in Cyrenaica: in order to build up essential stocks of petrol, ammunition and supplies.

I directed the New Zealand Division on Sidi Barrani, and

by the evening of 9 November, 4 Light Armoured Brigade had brushed aside the rearguards there and the advance to the frontier continued. Other enemy rearguards were overwhelmed on 10 November, and the next day a surprise attack carried out silently in the dark overran the defenders of Halfaya Pass. Capuzzo, Solum, and Bardia yielded without resistance, and thus by 11 November the Axis forces had been thrown out of Egypt.

2 New Zealand Division remained in the frontier area to reorganize, while 1 and 7 Armoured Divisions continued the pursuit. Tobruk was entered on 13 November, and after a further brush with the enemy at the Ain el Gazala defile, the Jebel el Akdar was reached. The Martuba airfields were in our hands on 15 November, just in time for aircraft to operate in support of a Malta convoy which sailed from Alexandria the following day.

My next objective was Benghazi. Intelligence reports suggested that the enemy would have great difficulty in getting his stores and material away from the town, and that shortage of petrol and transport might delay the evacuation of his personnel. If therefore we could reach Benghazi quickly, we might round up a considerable number of prisoners; moreover, I wanted to capture the port before the enemy had time to carry out heavy demolitions. I could not continue the pursuit with major forces owing to the maintenance situation and it was essential to wait until supplies had been built up forward. I therefore ordered 10 Corps to send light forces ahead in order to threaten Benghazi from the north and at the same time to cut the main coast road south of it. 4 Light Armoured Brigade operated along the coast road and a force of armoured cars was sent across the desert directed initially on Msus and Antelat. Subsequently the desert column was reinforced by an armoured regiment. Unfortunately heavy rain upset our plans and caused considerable delays to the desert column which gave the enemy some extra time to organize his withdrawal from Benghazi. Eventually the port was captured on 20 November.

My attention meanwhile turned to the Agheila position. The enemy was preparing to turn and face us in the area where twice before our forces had been brought to a halt. He was also digging in at Agedabia, which was the key to the approaches to the Agheila position.

7 Armoured Division quickly developed outflanking movements to the south of Agedabia, and the enemy withdrew by 23 November. He was evidently not strong enough to hold the place and at the same time to man the Agheila defences.

The next task of the Eighth Army was to face up to the enemy, build up the administrative situation while preparing to attack him and then once more drive him back to the west. I brought forward Headquarters 30 Corps to undertake this task. 10 Corps remained in Cyrenaica and I shall discuss its positioning later. 7 Armoured Division passed to command of 30 Corps.

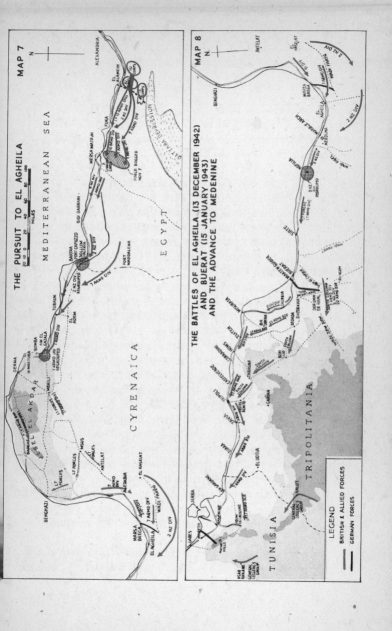

MAP 7

THE PURSUIT TO EL AGHEILA

MEDITERRANEAN SEA

20 10 0   20   40   60   80   100
MILES

CYRENAICA

EGYPT

QATTARA DEPRESSION

ALEXANDRIA

MAP 8

THE BATTLES OF EL AGHEILA (13 DECEMBER 1942)
AND BUERAT (15 JANUARY 1943)
AND THE ADVANCE TO MEDENINE

TRIPOLITANIA

TUNISIA

LEGEND

BRITISH & ALLIED FORCES

GERMAN FORCES

THE ACTIONS AT EL AGHEILA (13 DECEMBER 1942) AND BUERAT (15 JANUARY 1943) AND THE ADVANCE TO TRIPOLI

FORCING THE EL AGHEILA POSITION

The problem was now to turn the enemy out of the El Agheila position as quickly as possible before he had time to perfect the organization of his defences. I wanted to occupy the Agheila bottleneck myself, facing west, and thus ensure that the Axis forces would not hold the gateway to Cyrenaica a third time.

The first consideration was again administration. The bulk of our supplies had to be brought by road from Tobruk until the port of Benghazi could be got working at full pressure, and this task became a matter of urgent priority. At the same time the Royal Air Force demands for daily tonnage of stores were becoming very big and the estimate for these requirements in mid-December reached 1,400 tons per day, so that building up Army stocks for the advance was going to be a slow process. We had to ensure that the Royal Air Force could develop the maximum effort in its many tasks, all of which related directly or indirectly to the problem of removing the Axis forces from Africa, but it meant that I would be unable to start my operations against the Agheila position until mid-December.

My next anxiety was the reinforcement situation. I could not at this stage risk a battle involving heavy casualties. I would have to rely on artillery fire and air bombing, and keep my losses to a minimum.

I toured the forward area at the end of November in order to reconnoitre and make a plan. I was wondering whether, by bluff and manoeuvre on the open flank, I could frighten the enemy out of his positions. If it should appear to him that by making a stand to fight he would risk losing his whole force, he might withdraw. This would have suited me, as I could have taken possession of the bottleneck and fought him in the easier country to the west. As I shall explain later, I eventually decided to go all out to annihilate the enemy in his defences.

Meanwhile I worked out the plan of attack.

The Agheila position was naturally very strong. It covered the area of desert between the sea, just west of Marsa Brega and the Wadi Fareg—which formed a difficult obstacle running east and west. In the approaches to the position the 'going' was extremely bad, while for some distance to the south of the Wadi Fareg the ground was unsuitable for manoeuvre. A very wide detour would be necessary to outflank the position.

The enemy was known to be working hard at the defences, and he used immense quantities of mines to hinder our approach. Tripoli was still receiving heavy traffic and it was estimated that the German forces available in defence now disposed of up to 100 tanks and considerable numbers of anti-tank guns. Although reports during the first week in December indicated that Rommel was sending the Italians west, he showed no sign of evacuating the position. I decided that bluff would not remove him and planned to get behind his German forces and capture them.

My plan depended on finding a suitable route for 2 New Zealand Division to outflank the defensive system. This formation would move wide and cut the coast road well to the west of El Agheila. On the coast I would attack astride the road with 51 Division, and in the centre 7 Armoured Division would operate, with the lorried infantry brigade leading and with the armour positioned in rear. It was essential to conceal the outflanking move from the enemy, as he would be likely to withdraw rather than risk complete encirclement.

51

I eventually set 14 December as the date of the operation. Heavy artillery and air action against the enemy was to start two days earlier. I issued my orders on 11 December and a policy of large scale raids began at once. The raids were mistaken by the enemy for the main attack and unnerved him; in the early hours of 13 December he started to withdraw under cover of rearguards found by 90 Light Division. In spite of the great caution imposed on our troops by mines and booby traps of all kinds, we succeeded in following up closely, and at the end of the day 51 Division had penetrated the eastern sector of the defences. On the following day 7 Armoured Division took the lead and got into the rearguard just east of El Agheila itself and subsequently reached the causeway of the Marada fork.

The Desert Air Force did great execution on the coast road.

Meanwhile the New Zealand Division's outflanking movement was making fast progress. The Division started from El Haseiat, and passing well to the south of Wadi Farég, crossed the Marada track about 50 kilometres north of the oasis. It then moved north-west directed on Merduma and the coast road. The line of Wadi Rigel–Merduma was reached on 15 December after a remarkably rapid advance, and it was evident that most of the German armour and the rearguards of 90 Light Division were still to the east. The Germans were in a desperate plight with 7 Armoured Division advancing from the east and 2 New Zealand Division coming in behind. Fighting was intense and confused throughout 16 December. The enemy split up into small scattered groups and struggled through, suffering considerable losses in the process (including some 20 tanks and 500 prisoners) but uncertainty of the going and above all administrative restrictions had limited the size of the outflanking force, so that it was not strong enough to cut off the enemy completely.

The pursuit continued on 17 December, and next day the New Zealanders had a sharp engagement at Nofilia. By 19

December the enemy was withdrawing fast along the coast road, but in view of my administrative situation I was now able to follow up with light forces only.

The battle of El Agheila was at an end. Rommel's forces had been further weakened and I was in possession of the bottleneck which commanded the route into Cyrenaica and Egypt. The enemy had commenced to withdraw when our offensive intentions became clear, but his rearguards were severely mauled in the process. His morale had been further lowered and it was important to follow him up quickly, but the Eighth Army had covered 1,200 miles since 23 October and maintenance was our greatest problem.

CONSIDERATIONS AFFECTING THE ADVANCE TO THE BUERAT POSITION

When Rommel's forces retreated from El Agheila, his main bodies went back to the area of Buerat, which was the next suitable position on which to oppose our advance: a strong force including tanks remained at Sirte, and the enemy's intention was obviously to prevent Eighth Army from gaining contact with the Buerat position as long as possible.

The tempo of my operations was determined by administrative considerations. Before I could maintain major forces forward of Nofilia I had to build up stocks in the forward area, but 800 tons a day was still being brought by road from Tobruk, and Royal Air Force requirements had increased further with demands for all-weather runways for the heavy bombers. Tremendous efforts were made at Benghazi to improve the port facilities, as once our tonnage requirements could be handled there the transport locked up on the long road run to Tobruk could be switched to the shorter carry forward of Benghazi. Early in January 3,000 tons per day were being handled at Benghazi port and the situation began rapidly to improve.

We were not well placed for forward aerodromes, and the immediate consideration after El Agheila was the establishment of the Royal Air Force at Marble Arch and Merduma with forward squadrons at Nofilia. We also required to take Sirte and start work at once on airfields there, so that the Desert Air Force would be ready to give its customary scale of support in the Buerat battle.

I was also concerned with ensuring the correct balance in the rear areas and, in planning the next phase of our advance, was anxious to bring forward a corps to occupy the El Agheila position when 30 Corps moved on again to the west.

As a result of these considerations I ordered 30 Corps to halt 2 New Zealand Division in the Nofilia area, forward of which 4 Light Armoured Brigade operated alone. My orders provided that a forward base should be established at Sirte whence we would maintain contact with the enemy by means of armoured car patrols only. 7 Armoured Division was to remain about Marble Arch and 51 Division in the Agheila position cleaning up the area.

I decided to plan for the Buerat battle on the basis of ten days' heavy fighting using four divisions, and calculated that the necessary dumping would take some three weeks. I therefore intended to resume the offensive in mid-January.

ADVANCE OF LIGHT FORCES FROM NOFILIA TO BUERAT

Following the engagement at Nofilia on 18 December, the enemy moved westwards with great speed, covered by detachments from his armoured forces.

On 21 December contact was made with strong rear-guards at Sirte. Only after outflanking manoeuvres by armoured cars and artillery was the enemy compelled to evacuate the place, which we entered on 25 December. Two days later patrols had crossed the Wadi Tamet, and on 28 December they were overlooking the Wadi el Chebir. This implied that the enemy had withdrawn to his main position, which was reported to run from the coast at Maaten Giaber, south-west covering Gheddahia, and along Wadi Umm er Raml towards Bu Ngem.

1. 'Donald' was the mascot of the C.M.P.s of the 10th Armoured Division H.Q.
   He had been 'found' somewhere in the Nile Delta some months before
   and had been in the desert ever since. 24 October 1942.

2. One of the first pictures taken during the battle shows this group of Italian
   prisoners captured by the Highland Division. 26 October 1942.

3. German prisoners of the 90th Light Division captured by Australian units are escorted past an appropriate sign.

4. British trucks carrying infantry through a gap in an enemy minefield come under heavy shellfire. 27 October 1942.

Something for the troops in action to dream about! At their barracks British A.T.S. girls enjoy the luxury of their excellent swimming pool.

6. Filling a Crusader tank the hard way with a four-gallon can. Later in the campaign the Allies adopted the 'Jerry-can'.

7. This amusing sign in the Alemein lines is not so frivolous as it sounds. 27 October 1942.

8. The realities of war in the desert are brought home in this picture of a dead Italian lying beside a Breda gun. 29 October 1942.

9. Rather a macabre sign for one of the many blood banks which moved forward with the advance and saved many Allied lives. 29 October 1942.

10. The General Priest carries a 105mm. Howitzer on a self-propelled chassis. It has a high turn of speed and good manoeuvrability and proved particularly successful against the German 88mm. anti-tank guns. 2 November 1942.

11. One of the great pictures of the war. Australians storm a German strongpoint under cover of a smoke screen.

12. An effective shower except that most of the water was supposed to be saved by the lower tin!

13. After days of action with only water to drink, this Australian takes a long pull a a bottle of beer.

14. Sherman tanks advance to the front. 5 November 1942.

15. General Montgomery standing in front of his General Grant tank (Monty). This tank took the General from Alamein to the River Sangro.

16. A Sherman tank leaves a landing craft in the Sicily landings.

17. This fuel dump near Cesaro gives some idea of the vast amount of materials which were transported to Sicily to support the Allied invasion.

18. This Italian coastal gun-battery was p of the enemy defences which were deployed along parts of the Sicilian coast to prevent further Allied landing while the enemy troops withdrew to t mainland.

19. Highlanders unload parcels of cigarettes sent as a present from General Montgomery to the men of the Eighth Army.

By 29 December our patrol line was in position west of the enemy defences; Buerat and Bu Ngem were reported clear of enemy.

The Buerat position was not so strong naturally as Agheila, neither had the enemy had time to construct defences on the scale met previously. The wadis in the area, were, however, serious obstacles, particularly the Wadi Zem Zem. The main weakness of the position was that its southern flank did not rest on any natural obstacle and, by now, it was very apparent that the enemy had become extremely sensitive to out-flanking movements. He was therefore probably uncertain of his ability to hold the Buerat defences and therefore, as soon as he judged that the Eighth Army was resuming the offensive, he would begin to withdraw again. This would not have suited me because, primarily for administrative reasons, once I struck at Buerat I intended to drive straight through to Tripoli and open the port. If Rommel pulled back before I was ready I could not follow up, and I did not want him to have time for preparation of other major defences east of Tripoli itself. There was a good defensive position on the high ground from Homs to Tarhuna and beyond, which might prove difficult if developed, and my maintenance situation would not permit any delay in overcoming it.

I had always to take into account the possibility of the enemy withdrawing earlier than I hoped, and my plan was made to cover that eventuality. I estimated that I could resume the offensive on 15 January, and decided that I would not start before then whatever Rommel did, but that once the Army was set in motion, it would go straight to Tripoli. At the same time I gave orders which precluded the enemy suspecting any offensive intentions on my part. Only the armoured cars of 4 Light Armoured Brigade were facing the enemy, and the main bodies of 7 Armoured Division, which was responsible for the front, were to remain east of the Wadi Tamet, some 40 miles behind the line. The battle plan was subsequently worked out with the object of moving main bodies of assaulting formations forward at the last possible moment.

My intention at this stage was that 30 Corps should use four divisions in the assault together with a very strong force of tanks. 50 and 51 Divisions would attack astride the coast road, while 7 Armoured and 2 New Zealand Divisions would deliver the main thrust round the enemy's flank and drive in behind him. 22 Armoured Brigade I intended to keep in Army reserve in the centre, available to reinforce either thrust.

I intended to bring 10 Corps forward to the El Agheila position and subsequently to the Buerat area, so that I should preserve overall balance, and later leapfrog it through 30 Corps for operations west of Tripoli.

On 4 January ground and air reports both indicated that Italian formations were withdrawing from the Buerat position. This conformed to the events at Agheila. There was no sign of the Germans moving, however, and I continued the policy of standing well back and restricting our forward activity to armoured car patrols.

Dumping was going ahead well, when we sustained a major setback due to the weather. A gale raged from 4 to 6 January and created havoc at Benghazi port. Ships broke loose and charged about the harbour; heavy seas breached the breakwater and smashed into the inner harbour. Four ships were sunk, one of which contained 2,000 tons of ammunition, and great damage was done to lighters and tugs. The intake dropped from 3,000 tons per day to 1,000. This created a most awkward situation. We were thrown back on Tobruk and the necessity for a heavy daily lift by road from Cyrenaica to the forward area.

I was still determined to start the drive to Tripoli on 15 January. The enemy must not be given any longer respite, so I decided to modify my plan and accept the risks this would entail.

First, I decided not to bring 10 Corps forward but to take all its transport, both operational and administrative, and employ it in ferrying stores forward from Tobruk. This sacrificed my desire for correct balance, but was not a great risk. We faced a broken enemy, and we knew well that he could not recover sufficiently to launch out to the east again for some considerable time.

Secondly, I reduced the attacking forces of 30 Corps by leaving out 50 Division. This formation I was able to bring up to the Agheila area as custodian of the defensive positions there. The coastal thrust as planned would have had a hard task anyhow, and with only one division now available I ordered that the attack should not be pressed, but should aim at containing the enemy in the sector.

The main risk was in planning to reach Tripoli in ten days from the start of the operation. If I could not get the port in that time, I should be confronted with an extremely grave administrative situation. I decided to accept this risk in view of my great strength in tanks. By stripping 1 Armoured Division (10 Corps) I was able to concentrate 450 tanks for the battle. I was confident that this armoured force would offset the reduction in the number of divisions and, by careful handling, would ensure a speedy drive to the objective.

For the rest my plan of battle remained unchanged. 51 Division would press along the coast road, while 7 Armoured and 2 New Zealand Divisions would outflank the enemy and thrust towards Beni Ulid and Tarhuna. 22 Armoured Brigade would move between the main axes on Bir Dufan, and be ready to switch to either flank as required. A comprehensive air plan was drawn up, commencing with the customary domination of the Axis air force and culminating with bombing the enemy positions immediately prior to the attack.

I must mention the very unusual command set-up which was forced upon me in this battle. The plan involved two widely separated thrusts, with an armoured force moving between them under command of Army Headquarters. It was not possible for the one Corps Commander to direct both of these thrusts owing to the distance. The battle was going to require tremendous drive and energy to ensure reaching Tripoli in time, and a superior commander was essential on both flanks. As I had only one Corps Headquarters available for the action, I decided to command the coastal thrust myself from my Tactical Headquarters, leaving General Leese free to concentrate on the outflanking operations. I would move my Headquarters with 22 Armoured Brigade on the central axis.

I took special steps to work up the enthusiasm of the troops before the battle, and to impress upon them the need for firm determination that the attack would not stop until Tripoli was ours.

THE BATTLE OF BUERAT (15 January 1943) AND THE CAPTURE OF TRIPOLI (23 January 1943)

My final instructions for the Battle of Buerat provided for a due measure of caution to be exercised by the outflanking formations, as I wished to avoid heavy casualties to our tanks. It was necessary first to reconnoitre carefully the enemy anti-tank gun layout before rushing forward, because the defenders were thought to have some two hundred anti-tank guns and about twenty-five 88 millimetre pieces.

7 Armoured and 2 New Zealand Divisions moved off at 0715 hours 15 January. They soon made contact with 15 Panzer Division in the area Dor Umm er Raml, and destroyed fifteen German tanks in the ensuing action. The enemy fell back on the Wadi Zem Zem, and by evening Faschia had been secured and we were on the line of the wadi. On the coastal axis 51 Division attacked at 2230 hours, but was not heavily opposed as it transpired that 90 Light Division had started withdrawing after dusk. By the morning of 16 January our outflanking movement was through the main enemy position and had crossed the Wadi Zem Zem, while 51 Division was advancing on Gheddahia. I now ordered that the advance be conducted with great

resolution and the utmost speed; the caution imposed at the start of the operation was cancelled. In the afternoon tanks were encountered again near Sedada, but showed little fight. On the main road, our troops reached Churgia and 22 Armoured Brigade meanwhile advanced on Bir Dufan.

I gave orders on 17 January to 30 Corps to feel for the enemy's southern flank, making as if directed on Garian. Subsequently the thrust was to be developed towards Tripoli from the south as I wanted to play on the enemy's sensitiveness to outflanking movements, hoping he would weaken his Homs sector in order to strengthen the western flank. If the Tarhuna axis proved difficult and if the enemy weakened the Homs area to strengthen it further, I would drive hard from my eastern flank, releasing 22 Armoured Brigade into the plain of Tripoli along the coastal axis.

Steady progress was made on 17 January, but the ground slowed movement in the desert and, on the coast, mines and very skilful demolitions delayed us. By evening the southern column reached Beni Ulid, and on the right, we were only ten miles short of Misurata. Next day the enemy withdrawal continued, but on both flanks we lost contact owing to difficulties of the 'going' and to demolitions.

The advance was becoming sticky, and I was experiencing the first real anxiety I had suffered since assuming command of the Eighth Army. If I did not reach Tripoli within the ten days' time limit imposed by the administrative situation, I might have to face a most difficult decision: I would have to stop the advance and probably fall back to Buerat or even further, in order to maintain the supply of the Army. I was determined, therefore, to accelerate the pace of operations, and to give battle by night as well as by day, in order to break through the Homs–Tarhuna position and secure my objective. I ordered attacks on both axes to be put in by moonlight. I issued very strong instructions regarding the quickening of our efforts, and made clear what I expected of commanders and the troops. On 19 January progress greatly improved; pressure was being developed on Tarhuna and 51 Division entered Homs. I had 22 Armoured Brigade at Zliten, still under my command, waiting for the right moment to release it. The Desert Air Force had a most successful day, and indeed it took a constant and heavy toll of the enemy throughout this action.

I received reports that the Ramcke parachutists had been transferred from the Homs front across to Tarhuna, and this decided me to adopt the plan already contemplated of striking a hard blow on the right flank, and launching 22 Armoured Brigade through to Castelverde and Tripoli.

By the evening of 21 January, 51 Division had forced the enemy back from the hills about Corradini, and 22 Armoured Brigade had been brought up west of Homs. But the pace was still too slow, in spite of my insistence on the urgency of the operation; the difficulty was that the demolitions on the road had been most skilfully related to the ground, so that it was often impossible even for tracked vehicles to by-pass them owing to soft sand and deep ravines.

On 22 January I ordered 22 Armoured Brigade to pass through 51 Division and to force its way forward to Tripoli. By 1400 hours the brigade was held up by rearguards and demolitions west of Castelverde and was unable to get round them; owing to traffic blocks, there was only one company of infantry forward to assist, and I therefore ordered a battalion of 51 Division to ride to the front on Valentine tanks and to attack on arrival. This involved a night attack, and the armour was to follow through by moonlight. Meanwhile progress had been made on the left flank, and the southern column was only seventeen miles from Tripoli. It seemed that the city must now fall, and it was with very great satisfaction that I received reports that it had been entered from the east and south in the early hours of 23 January.

By dark the enemy were thirty miles west of Tripoli and I ordered the pressure to be continued to Zuara, which was near the Tunisian border, 7 Armoured Division was to follow up. Meanwhile the rest of 30 Corps was grouped round Tripoli, while preparations were made for the next phase of operations.

In three months exactly, we had advanced 1,400 miles and Tripoli, the last Italian colonial city, the prize which had so long eluded the Desert Army, had been captured at last. The damage in the town was not great, but the port was extensively demolished. Quays, wharves and installations were badly destroyed, and the harbour entrance blocked completely. All our energies were concentrated on getting it working again, and indeed this was achieved with remarkable speed and reflected very great credit on the Royal Navy and Army staffs and units concerned. On 3 February the first ship entered the harbour, and a complete convoy was berthed within three days. By 10 February, over 2,000 tons were being handled per day in the port.

The problem now was to build up the maintenance resources of the Army before advancing into Tunisia. Meanwhile I established my Headquarters in a field, four miles outside Tripoli City, and kept my army in the fields and in the desert around it. In Tripoli there were palaces, villas and buildings galore, but I could not have the soldiers getting soft. It was necessary to safeguard their hardness and efficiency for the tasks which lay ahead.

During our stay in Tripoli the Prime Minister, Mr Winston Churchill, paid a visit to the Eighth Army. A ceremonial march past was arranged in the main square, and it was a brave and moving spectacle when he inspected the troops who had fought their long way from Egypt to this fair city.

SOME REFLECTIONS ON THE CAMPAIGN IN EGYPT AND LIBYA

There are some aspects of the conduct of the campaign in Egypt and Libya upon which it is interesting to comment.

Twice our Desert Army had advanced to El Agheila, and twice it had been forced to withdraw into Egypt. This time I was determined to ensure that there could never be any question of another reverse in the Western Desert, and never

61

any possibility of a recurrence of what was then becoming known in the Eighth Army as the 'annual swan' between Egypt and El Agheila. As we approached El Agheila I sensed a feeling of depression, particularly among some of those officers who had participated in our previous offensives and withdrawals; I did not feel depressed at the prospect myself.

I have already mentioned that to me there was a radical difference in the circumstances of the third advance of our Desert Forces to Benghazi and beyond, as compared with previous occasions, because Rommel had been decisively beaten in battle and had been thrown back into Tripolitania as a result of his defeat. Previously he had withdrawn mainly of his own volition, and perhaps primarily for administrative reasons. The full fruits of victory cannot be gathered until the enemy has been defeated in battle. In November and December 1942 the enemy was not in a position to make any effective speedy recovery or to turn to the attack, because he had been beaten and his morale shaken. He was relentlessly pursued westwards. In the engagements after El Alamein, he was quickly set upon and forced to continue his retreat, principally by outflanking manoeuvres which he had been quite unable to withstand.

I did not rely, however, on the effects of Rommel's defeat to ensure that he would not try again to invade Egypt. From the time the pursuit from El Alamein began I gave much thought to the problem. I planned to preserve the strategic balance of the Army by maintaining, in a series of chosen areas, a force which would ensure against the effects of any local failure or surprise being turned to important advantage by the enemy. If then Rommel should succeed in halting our advance and subsequently continue to build up his forces for a renewed attempt on the Nile Delta, I would be able to defeat his purpose.

I decided that the first essential safeguard against another Axis recovery was the positioning of a strong mobile force in the general area to the south-east of the Jebel Akdar, centring on Tmimi and Ain el Gazala. I therefore left 10 Corps in that area, using 7 Armoured Division to continue the pursuit to Agheila. I then brought 30 Corps forward for the Agheila battle. As long as I had 10 Corps poised in the Tmimi area, Rommel could not return to the Egyptian frontier, even if he did find the means to turn and attack us again. 10 Corps blocked the road axis to Tobruk and beyond, and if by-passed to the south would lie on the flank of any overland route the Germans might select across the waterless desert.

Later, when we stood before the Agheila position, my first concern was to acquire its defences for myself. Whoever was established firmly in the Agheila bottleneck held the gateway to Cyrenaica. This was an immensely strong position and, once we could garrison it, there would never again be any question of the Germans returning to the east. For this reason, when Agheila fell my intention was to bring 10 Corps forward to occupy it while 30 Corps advanced to Buerat and subsequently to Tripoli. After forcing the Buerat position, I intended to pull 10 Corps forward to garrison it, while 30 Corps captured Tripoli. I would then leave 30 Corps at Tripoli to reorganize, while 10 Corps 'leapfrogged' through, leading the way into Tunisia. I was prevented from this by the maintenance situation which arose as a result of the storm on 4–6 January, and was obliged to advance leaving only one division on the Agheila position behind me. Admittedly there was little or no risk involved in this, but nevertheless when we went forward from Agheila we were not theoretically 'balanced' in our rear dispositions even though the state of the enemy made it permissible to neglect the full application of this principle.

I was loath to depart from my intentions for 10 Corps at that time; a battle is always fought with more confidence, particularly a mobile battle in the desert, if it is staged in front of a secure base: should the enemy succeed in catching the assaulting formations at a disadvantage, they can reorganize at that base and avoid being overwhelmed and thrown into confusion.

I have elaborated above on my conception of 'balance' in the strategic aspect. It is of equal importance on the battle-field, as has already been apparent in this story.

It is interesting to conjecture why Rommel failed to stand and fight at Agheila. It was the first defensive position at which he had the opportunity to face our advance with any chance of success, yet we turned him out of it with comparative ease. The Agheila position was immensely strong and very heavily mined. If the available German armour had been positioned on its southern flank, north of Marada, it might have been very difficult for me. My outflanking movement was necessarily weak owing to maintenance restrictions, and it was launched into difficult country. My whole force was stretched administratively, relying largely on Tobruk, some 450 miles by road in the rear.

I believe Rommel was unable to fight at Agheila because his own administrative situation was so extended. He was dependent on a road link back to Tripoli, and his losses in transport and shortage of petrol made this distance prohibitive.

Having given up Agheila, it is surprising that he decided to stand at Buerat. The Buerat position was not naturally strong, nor had it been developed into a sound defensive system. Moreover it could readily be outflanked. In rear covering Tripoli, was an immensely superior defensive position—the escarpment running from Homs on the coast through Tarhuna and Garian. If the energy expended on Buerat had instead been applied to the Homs–Tarhuna area I do not think the Eighth Army would have reached Tripoli in January. Not only was this area much more favourable to the defence than Buerat, but my administrative situation would have made it almost impossible for me to follow up even with armoured cars, had the Axis forces gone straight back there from Agheila. They would have had a considerable period of relative immunity from our attentions in which to prepare against a renewal of our offensive. I can think of no sound military reason for Rommel's decision to stop at Buerat. I believe that Mussolini ordered it and that Rommel could not disobey until our advance gave him the excuse. By then it was too late.

The reinforcements made available to Rommel during his withdrawal enabled him to retain the identity of the German formations present at El Alamein. At first sight it seems strange that formations such as 15 and 21 Panzer Divisions continued to oppose us, after their experiences in October and November. The German tank strength began to recover to some extent at Agheila. It was evident that up to the time Tripoli was captured, the Axis Powers made full use of the port to send assistance to their hard-pressed forces. As Rommel subsequently withdrew into Tunisia, he was able to demand for the German Africa Corps its share of resources made available in that theatre. Because of this we continued to meet old opponents right through to the bitter end of the campaign, and it used to be said that Eighth Army would be pursuing '90 Light' till the end of time.

Before continuing the narrative of events, mention may here be made of some of the special problems which confronted us in Tripolitania.

I have frequently referred to the administrative factor from the time we left El Alamein. The tempo of operations was primarily governed by the speed with which petrol, ammuntion, Air Force requirements, and all the necessary stores and materials could be brought forward in sufficient quantities to support the fighting troops. It is important to grasp the distances with which the administrative machine had to contend. From Cairo to Tripoli is 1,600 miles by road; with GHQ at the former and the leading troops at the latter, it was as if GHQ were in London and the leading troops in Moscow, with only one road joining them. After the big storm of 4–6 January, the bulk of our stores was brought from Tobruk to Buerat by road, a distance of 700 miles: equivalent to being disposed at Vienna and drawing stores in London, with only one road available. On arrival in

Tripoli, until the port was functioning, all requirements had to come from Benghazi, again about 700 miles by road. I planned to continue at first to maintain the Army by road from Benghazi, so that the intake at Tripoli port could be stored as reserve stocks. As soon as the reserves were adequate for the resumption of the advance in strength, I would close the road link to Benghazi and maintain the Army from Tripoli.

The problem of aerodromes in Tripolitania was an important one. When fighting in Egypt or Cyrenaica there was never any shortage of airfield sites. Both sides had fought over the ground several times, and had constructed many landing grounds, the locations of which were well known. This did not apply in Tripolitania where airfields were scarce and likely to be ploughed up and mined: as in the case of Marble Arch and Merduma. To rehabilitate old sites and construct new ones as the advance continued took time, but until this was done the Desert Air Force was forced to operate from locations in the rear with consequent limitations of range and endurance over the battlefield. I had to ensure, therefore, that due provision was made for airfield construction, and at the same time see that the leading troops did not outrun the air cover. There were very rare occasions when I had to decide between halting the pursuit or continuing without air cover for the leading elements. For example, the importance of reaching Agedabia and the Agheila position quickly was such that I accepted for a short period lack of cover in the forward area, and the enemy air force caused us certain casualties at that stage on the Benghazi–Agedabia road. But in any but special and rare circumstances, I am sure it is unsound to deny the troops fighter protection.

The capture of Tripoli presented us with all the problems of dealing with a large civilian population. I imposed very strict military discipline when we arrived, but was ready to relax it as the situation warranted. The Chief Civil Affairs Officer entered Tripoli with my Headquarters.

CHAPTER SEVEN

THE ADVANCE INTO TUNISIA AND THE BATTLES OF MEDENINE (6 MARCH 1943) AND OF THE MARETH LINE (20 MARCH 1943)

THE ADVANCE INTO TUNISIA

As a result of the Anglo-American Conference at Casablanca on 14 January, it had been decided to unify the command of the Allied Forces in North Africa, and General Eisenhower became the Supreme Allied Commander. General Alexander was appointed his Deputy, and Air Marshal Tedder took over command of all the air forces in the Mediterranean. This facilitated the co-ordination of Allied effort, and in particular made possible the concentration of all available air resources when required at any vital point. General Alexander visited me in the middle of February, and it was subsequently agreed by the Supreme Commander that priority should be given to getting the Eighth Army into the open maritime plain of Tunisia towards Sfax and Sousse.

Reverting to the immediate problems confronting us at Tripoli, my object was to push the enemy back to his next defensive position: the Mareth Line. I would have to drive in his covering troops, 'lean' up against his defences and make a plan to pierce them. I had also to secure the necessary centres of communications and lateral roads, and seize the forward airfields: particularly those about Medenine.

Owing to administrative restrictions, I advanced west of Tripoli with 7 Armoured Division only, which then included 4 Light Armoured Brigade. 2 New Zealand and 51 Divisions reorganized in the Tripoli area.

Following the fall of Tripoli on 23 January, the Axis forces continued their withdrawal westwards covered by rearguards of 90 Light and 164 Divisions. On 25 January

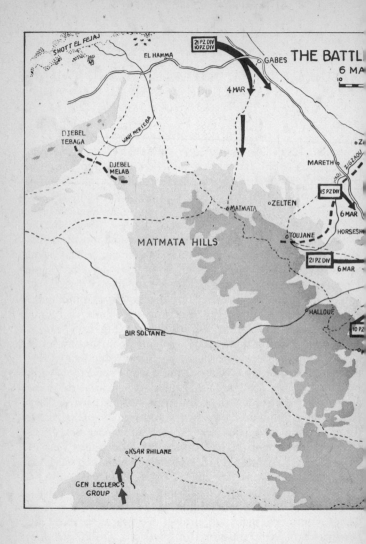

SHOTT EL FEJAJ

EL HAMMA

GABES

21 PZ DIV
10 PZ DIV

THE BATTL

6 MA

4 MAR

DJEBEL
TEBAGA

OUAD MERTEBA

DJEBEL
MELAB

MARETH

Z

WADI ZIGZAOU

oMATMATA

oZELTEN

15 PZ DIV

6 MAR

MATMATA HILLS

oTOUJANE

HORSESHL

21 PZ DIV

6 MAR

HALLOUF

10 PZ

BIR SOLTANE

oKSAR RHILANE

GEN LECLERC'S
GROUP

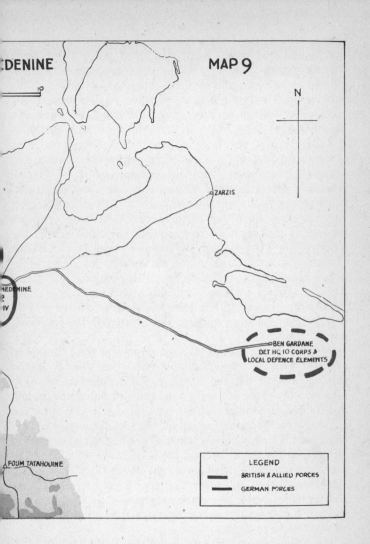

MAP 9

N

ZARZIS

MEDENINE
2
IV

BEN GARDANE
DET HQ 10 CORPS &
LOCAL DEFENCE ELEMENTS

FOUM TATAHOUINE

LEGEND

BRITISH & ALLIED FORCES

GERMAN FORCES

our troops entered Zavia and two days later were just short of Zuara, while inland El Uotia was reached. At Zuara the enemy stiffened his rearguards and our light forces were much hampered by wet weather and bad 'going'. We did not capture the place until 31 January; on the same day Nalut was reported clear, and by 4 February the last of the Italian Empire was in our hands. Meanwhile reports were being received of enemy activity in the Mareth Line, where the defences were being hurriedly developed and strengthened.

Once across the Tunisian border the enemy resistance stiffened further, and it became apparent that he intended to impose the maximum delay on our approach to his Mareth positions. His first main outpost was Ben Gardane, a fortified village to the south-west of which 15 Panzer Division was located. In order to give confidence and provide balance, I moved 22 Armoured Brigade close behind the front, while 7 Armoured Division prepared to tackle Ben Gardane from the south-east. Unfortunately another spell of heavy rain delayed our plans; from 10 February for several days the desert became a quagmire and made operations impossible, but on 15 February the weather cleared and we entered Ben Gardane without great difficulty the following day.

My next move was to take the important road centres of Medenine and Foum Tatahouine and the airfields at the former place. I decided to bring 51 Division forward, in view of the degree of enemy resistance to our advance, and this formation together with 7 Armoured Division launched an attack on Medenine, which fell on 17 February. The next day Foum Tatahouine was taken. I now had the co-operation of General Leclerc's force in the battle zone; this force had made a remarkable drive across the desert from Lake Chad, and placed itself under my orders. I gave it the task of moving from Nalut along the escarpment to Ksar Rhilane and of subsequently operating eastwards to threaten the enemy's western flank.

I had now secured the key approaches to the Mareth Line,

and when ready could close up to it and decide upon my plan.

The port at Tripoli was working well, and soon as much as 3,500 tons were being discharged there in one day—a remarkable achievement. The tank replacement programme was also satisfactory. I hoped to have three armoured brigades and two Valentine regiments up to strength by 20 March, to give me a total of some 550 tanks.

I planned to start operations against the Mareth defences about 20 March. I should require 10 Corps forward for the operation and expected to have 1 Armoured, 4 Indian, and 50 Divisions concentrated in the Tripoli area by 16 March.

As planning was beginning for the Mareth battle, events elsewhere in Tunisia were destined to affect the Eighth Army's intentions. On 15 February the enemy launched a strong attack against 2 United States Corps in the Gafsa sector of western Tunisia. The Americans withdrew towards Tebessa, and by 20 February the situation had become very grave. The enemy penetration was threatening to outflank Allied positions to the north, and unless this was halted quickly it seemed 5 British Corps would have to withdraw. General Alexander sent me an urgent request for help, urging me to exert all possible pressure on the enemy on my front in an effort to draw him off the Tebessa drive.

Eighth Army was administratively not ready to operate major forces in southern Tunisia, but this was an occasion when risks had to be taken, and I at once planned to intensify our drive towards the Mareth Line on the coast axis, and also to push Leclerc's force north from Ksar Rhilane. The enemy had weakened his Mareth front in order to strengthen the thrust through Gafsa, and there was always a chance that by forceful and energetic action I might frighten him out of his Mareth position. Though I was weak myself in front, urgent action was necessary if we were to help the Americans.

On 24 February four fighter wings were operating from the Medenine–Ben Gardane area. I ordered 7 Armoured and

51 Divisions to keep up the pressure, the former in the coastal sector, the latter on the main Gabes road. This involved a considerable risk, because if the enemy broke off the Tebessa attack and could regroup quickly against the Eighth Army, I should be in an awkward situation. I had only two divisions forward, with my main administrative area under development at Ben Gardane, and the nearest reserve division (2 New Zealand) was still back near Tripoli.

My leading formations accelerated and strengthened their action against the outer defences of the Mareth Line, and in the last days of February it was clear that this had achieved the desired result. Rommel broke off his attack against the Americans and reports of regrouping of enemy forces began to reach my Headquarters.

On 27 February 15 Panzer Division was located on my front, having been absent during the Tebessa offensive, and 21 Panzer Division was also reported to be moving south again.

It looked indeed as if my anxieties were justified, and that Rommel had decided to strike at the Eighth Army while there was an opportunity of dealing a crushing blow at its leading divisions. He could guess how very stretched we had become, and if he could overwhelm my forward area before I could get more troops forward, and overrun my dumps at Ben Gardane, he could cause a major setback to my plans and gain valuable time for dealing with other sectors of the Allied front in Tunisia.

The enemy tank strength was improving for 'Tiger' tanks were now being reported by First Army and he had 10 Panzer Division in Tunisia. I did not think that Rommel would bring all three armoured divisions against me, but in the event this is what happened.

As soon as the Tebessa thrust was called off by the enemy, the Americans began to advance: out of contact with the Germans who pulled back to their original line. This, together with the reports of February indicating the return of 15 and 21 Panzer Divisions to my front, confirmed the enemy's intentions.

I initiated emergency measures to regain balance and to prepare for an enemy attack. 2 New Zealand Division was ordered to Medenine at once. 8 Armoured Brigade was resting near Tripoli, and had been 'stripped' of its equipment; it was re-equipped with tanks then arriving at Tripoli in readiness for the arrival of 2 Armoured Brigade, and was sent forward. Together with 22 Armoured Brigade and eighty Valentines of 23 Armoured Brigade, I estimated that by 4 March I should have some 400 tanks at the front. By that date, 2 New Zealand Division would have joined 7 Armoured and 51 Divisions. I should then be ready for any move by Rommel, and would be so strong and well positioned that I might give him a rude shock and inflict on him heavy casualties: in fact pave the way for my own offensive against the Mareth Line, in the same manner as the Alam Halfa battle had facilitated the victory at El Alamein.

But I would not be ready until 4 March, and during the period 28 February–3 March the Eighth Army was unbalanced. In driving on to assist the west Tunisian front I had taken serious risks. Rommel had been forced to pull out and was now concentrating against me. The first days of March were an anxious period, during which all the signs of the impending enemy attack were apparent and it remained to be seen whether the enemy could strike before our arrangements to receive him were completed. This was my second period of great anxiety since the advance began.

On 3 March the enemy operated against 51 Division with infantry and tanks in a probing attack which was dealt with very quickly.

During 4 and 5 March, Rommel's intentions were made clear. Air reconnaissance reported heavy movement, including tanks, in the mountains west of Medenine. We began to identify three separate armoured columns, one facing us in the Mareth area (which we knew was 15 Panzer Division), one in the mountains making as if to come upon Medenine from the west and south-west (later identified as 10 Panzer

Division), and a third which was also suspected to be in the mountains (and which was 21 Panzer Division).

But Rommel had by now missed his opportunity. My dispositions were complete by the evening of 4 March. In addition to 400 tanks, I had over 500 anti-tank guns in position round Medenine and had brought a nucleus of 10 Corps Headquarters to Ben Gardane to organize local defence of the administrative area there.

We had no wire and no minefields, but the positioning of the infantry and siting of the anti-tank guns, together with the strong reserves of armour, gave our defences great strength, and I was confident that we would repulse the enemy and give him a sharp lesson.

THE BATTLE OF MEDENINE, 6 March 1943

On 5 March Rommel, by now a sick man, addressed his troops in the mountains overlooking our positions and told them that if they did not take Medenine and force the Eighth Army to withdraw, the days of the Axis forces in North Africa were numbered.

The next day the enemy attack began. When the early morning mist dispersed, a formidable array of tanks bore down upon our positions and it was clear that the main thrust was being made from the west towards the Tadjera feature, immediately north of Medenine, on 7 Armoured Division sector. By 1000 hours all attacks had been held and 21 enemy tanks destroyed. At 1430 hours, 15, 21, and part of 10 Panzer Divisions attacked again with infantry and were speedily beaten off. Our positions remained firm and steady and were not penetrated. There was a total of four main attacks during the day, apart from those which were broken up by concentrations of artillery fire before they had properly developed.

After dark the enemy withdrew: the battle was over. It had been a model defensive engagement and a great triumph for the infantry and the anti-tank gun. Only one squadron of our tanks was actually engaged in the fighting, and we lost no tanks. Fifty-two knocked out enemy tanks were left on the battlefield, and all but seven (dealt with by the tank squadron) had fallen to our anti-tank guns. Without wire or mines our infantry, with strong artillery support, had repulsed an attack by three Panzer divisions and incurred only minor losses in the process. Very great care had been taken in positioning our anti-tank guns, and it should be noted that they were sited to kill tanks at point-blank range: and not to defend the infantry.

Having disposed of Rommel, I continued my preparations for breaking through the Mareth Line and forcing my way into the maritime plain beyond Gabes.

The Mareth Line was originally constructed by the French to protect Tunisia against attack by the Italians from Libya. The main defences stretched for approximately 22 miles from the sea near Zarat to the Matmata Hills in the west. These hills are very broken and, except for a few tracks running through narrow passes, form a barrier to wheeled transport and give command over the whole western end of the position. At the eastern end of the line, the defences were based on the Wadi Zigzaou, which had been widened and deepened to form a tank obstacle, and which was covered along its whole length by a complicated system of concrete and steel pillboxes and gun emplacements.

Additional work had been done on the line since the Franco-German armistice by Italians under German supervision. Anti-tank ditches, wire, and protective minefields had been added, and a switch line was constructed following the Wadi Merteba between Djebel Melab and Djebel Tebaga, to the south-west of El Hamma. The designers of the line had apparently considered it impossible to outflank it west of the Matmata Hills as the ground was extremely difficult, and because any outflanking operation would involve a journey of at least 150 miles over waterless desert before the switch

75

line in front of El Hamma was reached. It was said that the French had tried an exercise in outflanking the line, using a small transport column for the task, and that all the lorries except two broke down owing to the impossibly bad 'going'. The French had therefore contented themselves with employing Arab irregulars to guard the few tracks leading into the Matmata Hills.

In view of our greatly superior transport I was not prepared to accept the French opinion, and as far back as December, when pondering on the problem of the Mareth Line, decided to have the area concerned reconnoitred. At that time I was at Marble Arch and had at my disposal the 'Long Range Desert Group' which was admirably suited to the task. So it was that in January 1943, while in Tripoli, I received a full report on the possibility of finding a way round the Mareth defences, and although it was apparent that very great difficulty would be experienced in crossing the country, it was not impossible, and I was confident that with our vehicles and experience a route could be found which would enable us to outflank the enemy.

An added problem at Mareth was the difficulty in establishing contact with the main defensive system, which was protected by a series of very well sited outpost and covering positions, particularly to the west of the main road running north into Mareth. Moreover, I suspected that I should find another position in rear, covering the bottleneck between the sea and the Shott el Fejaj, and this in fact proved to be the case.

On the coastal sector the enemy manned the Mareth defences primarily with Italians. 90 Light Division was west of the main road, and in the hills on the western flank 164 Division was located. The armour was in reserve in the rear.

Back in mid-February, before the Axis thrust at Gafsa and its sequel at Medenine, I had started studying the problem of breaching the Mareth Line, and had decided on an outline plan, subject to the normal modifications which subsequent reconnaissance might render desirable. I would attack on the coast with 30 Corps, striking at the Italians holding that area; meanwhile I would send 2 New Zealand Division, heavily reinforced, round the western flank to break in behind the Matmata massif. I would hold 10 Corps in reserve with two armoured divisions and 4 Light Armoured Brigade ready to tackle the Gabes bottleneck. A very great part would be played by the air striking forces in this battle, as we should have call on the combined resources of the Allies in North Africa.

I have mentioned that I planned to launch this operation about 20 March. 10 Corps was due to have concentrated forward by 16 March, and by that time the administrative situation would have become sufficiently strong to support a major offensive operation.

I have explained how Medenine and Foum Tatahouine, the key approaches to the Mareth Line, had been taken in the middle of February, and how operations had continued by 7 Armoured and 51 Divisions driving in the enemy covering troops and thus getting to grips with the main defensive positions.

Following the Battle of Medenine the process was continued.

On the western flank General Leclerc's force was providing an essential screen, which evidently caused the enemy considerable anxiety. On 10 March Rommel suddenly delivered a heavy attack with armoured cars, artillery, and aircraft against the French column, apparently intending to destroy it. But Leclerc stood firm and, ably assisted by the Desert Air Force, drove off the attack in which the enemy lost twelve armoured cars, twelve guns, and some forty vehicles. This fine performance prevented the enemy reconnoitring towards the New Zealand concentration area.

On night 16/17 March I began operations designed as the immediate preliminaries to the Mareth Battle. I now intended to destroy the last covering positions and also to mislead the enemy about the direction of the main thrust. These operations were completely successful except in the case of the Guards Brigade which attacked the 'Horseshoe' feature, a ring of hills at the south-west end of the Mareth defences, dominating the main road to Mareth. The brigade ran into most intensive minefields; Tellermines, anti-personnel mines, and 'S' mines were almost touching in some areas, and it was impossible to get carriers or vehicles forward. Heavy hand-to-hand fighting ensued, and the enemy suffered severe casualties, as did our own troops who were withdrawn at daylight.

Other local operations were carried out on the night 17/18 March, after which everything was ready for the battle. I let the whole front quieten down. General Freyberg's out-flanking column, temporarily designated New Zealand Corps, was lying concealed ready to begin its long march round to the west. Minor patrol activity continued on 19 March with the object of drawing the enemy's attention away from the right flank, where my initial blow was to fall.

In my discussion with General Alexander emphasis had been made on the importance of 2 United States Corps attempting to pin down the enemy on the Gafsa sector to prevent reserves being drawn from there to the Mareth Line, and also to re-establish the dumps at Gafsa itself, from which the Eighth Army was to draw when it advanced. 2 United States Corps launched an offensive on 17 March and captured Gafsa, and in the fighting round El Guettar was opposed by 10 Panzer Division and some Italian for-mations. This American advance was eventually stopped near Maknassy and El Guettar, but assisted our operations above all by containing 10 Panzer Division.

THE BATTLE OF THE MARETH LINE, 20 March 1943

20 March was a fine clear day, which was particularly welcome as it enabled us to take air photographs to check the enemy battery positions; we had had bad weather for three days during which air photography had been impos-sible.

My plan, which I explained personally to officers down

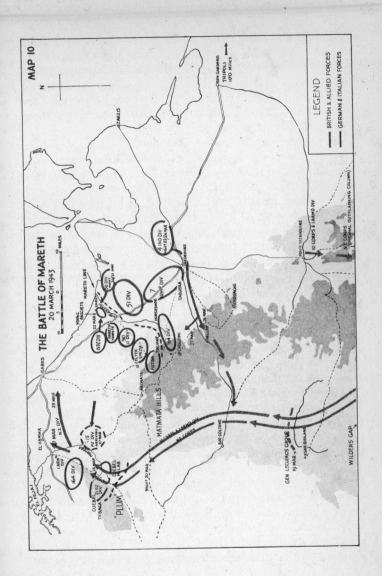

MAP 10

THE BATTLE OF MARETH
20 MARCH 1943

N

MILES
10   5   0   10
MARETH LINE

LEGEND
BRITISH & ALLIED FORCES
GERMAN & ITALIAN FORCES

GABES

YOUNG FASCISTS

51 DIV

90 (LT) DIV
TRIESTE

15 DIV

22 MAR & 22/23 MAR

50 DIV
NIGHT 20/21 MAR

50 DIV
NIGHT 20/21 MAR

MARETH

ZELTEN
SPEZIA

ZARAT

PISTOIA

CRESSINI

TOUJANE

HORSESHOE

164 DIV

PLUM

DJEBEL
TEBAGA

DJEBELL
2152 DIV
NIGHT 20 MAR

EL HAMMA

164 DIV

1 ARM
DIV

NZ DIV
29 MAR

27 MAR

15
NZ DIV

DJEBEL
MELAB
26 MAR

DJEBELL
MELAB

MATMATA HILLS

KSAR RHILANE

BIR SOLTANE

DORRIS & LARHO DIV
NZ CORPS

NIGHT 20 MAR

GEN LECLERCS GROUP
19 MAR

WILDERS GAP

27 MAR

TADJERA

TOUJANE

HALLOUF

4 IND DIV
NIGHT 23/24 MAR

80TH DIV

MEDENINE

TADJERA

KIRCHAOUINE

27 MAR

FROM TATAHOUINE

10 CORPS & LARHO DIV

NZ CORPS
(ORIGINAL OUTFLANKING COLUMN)

ZANZIS

FROM GABRINE
TRIPOLI
100 MILES

to the rank of Lieutenant-Colonel throughout the Army, depended on a major attack on the eastern end of the Mareth Line together with a very powerful outflanking movement. I did not think the enemy was strong enough to withstand both blows, and if he concentrated against one then I would succeed in the other. The final objective for the battle I gave as Sfax and ordered that operations would continue without pause until Sfax was secured.

30 Corps was to deliver the coastal attack using 50 Division and 23 Armoured Brigade; these formations would pass through 51 Division which was then holding the eastern sector of the front.

The New Zealand Corps consisting, in addition to 2 New Zealand Division, of 8 Armoured Brigade, Leclerc's force, an armoured car regiment and a medium artillery regiment, was to carry out the turning movement round the enemy's western flank. The Corps was to move towards Nalut, in a wide sweep to the south, reaching the escarpment by way of Wilder's Gap (as we called it), then swinging northwards to pass through Ksar Rhilane to the El Hamma switch line, and so reach its objective: the Gabes area.

10 Corps was to be in Army reserve, and its two armoured divisions were initially sited to guard the central sector between the two major thrusts. The Corps would be ready to exploit success.

A very heavy weight of air support was made available for the operation.

The attack by 50 Division was to commence at 2230 hours on 20 March. The New Zealand Corps was to advance 40 miles to an assembly area during the night 19/20 March, lie concealed all day 20 March, and continue by night marches until discovered by the enemy. In this deception we were unsuccessful for I had reason to believe that the enemy discovered the outflanking move earlier than I had hoped and I directed General Freyberg to continue marching by day throughout 20 March. This acceleration would, I hoped, distract attention from the coastal sector, and give a greater chance of success to the operations of 50 Division.

The New Zealand Corps pressed on throughout 20 March. It was a great relief to me to hear of its steady progress over the appallingly difficult ground. Very great credit is due to this force of some 27,000 men and 200 tanks in overcoming the truly enormous difficulties of terrain as well as enemy action on the approach march to the El Hamma switch line. Leclerc's force had a stiff task in pushing the enemy off a difficult wadi north of Ksar Rhilane, and a formidable engineering feat then faced the sappers in preparing tracks across the only possible crossing place some 100 yards wide. This and all other difficulties were surmounted so that by last light on 20 March, General Freyberg's troops were only a few miles short of the bottleneck (known to us as 'Plum') between the Djebel Tebaga and Djebel Melab, where the enemy switch line was located.

Preceded by a tremendous barrage of artillery, the attack of 50 Division started according to plan. The assaulting troops crossed the Wadi Zigzaou to capture three major strong points on the northern bank. The wadi proved to be every bit as difficult an obstacle as we had feared; there was a certain amount of water in it, and the banks had been cut away sheer; the enemy's guns and mortars had registered on it accurately, and our troops met intense enfilade fire from the flanks. 50 Division did well in securing its objectives for the strong points were very well found and were protected by wire, minefields, and all the adjuncts of well developed static defences. At dawn on 21 March, however, there were still pockets of enemy holding out in some of the defences, and the sappers found extreme difficulty in continuing their work of trying to construct crossing places for infantry carriers, supporting weapons, and tanks. A few Valentine tanks did succeed in crossing the wadi, but the going was impossible for wheels. Our tank losses were considerable.

The situation on 21 March on the coastal sector was that

we had gained a foothold in the Mareth defences, and the 'dog-fight' was on.

We held all our gains throughout 21 March, and that night there was another heavy artillery programme under cover of which the bridgehead was expanded both laterally and in depth. But the German reserves were now beginning to arrive and fighting increased in intensity. On 22 March we experienced more heavy rain which had a very serious effect on the operation; we had still failed to make a satisfactory crossing over the wadi, and the rain completely spoilt the preliminary work which had by then been done. During the morning it became apparent that 15 Panzer Division was forming up to deliver a counter-attack against our bridgehead, and the Desert Air Force alerted the light bombers in order to deal with this threat. But owing to the rain the aircraft were unable to take off, and during the afternoon the German blow fell. Much of the ground we had gained was recaptured by the enemy because we were not able to withstand his strong force of tanks, for conditions had made it impossible for us to get our own anti-tank guns across the wadi to oppose the German armour. It transpired that the German reinforcements against our bridgehead consisted not only of 15 Panzer Division, but also included a regiment of 90 Light Division and the Ramcke parachutists.

At 0200 hours on the night 22/23 March the full implications of the situation on the coastal sector were evident. The results of the German counter attack were serious but I knew that his reserves were now definitely committed on the eastern flank. I realized that it would be very costly to persist in our attacks there, and I therefore made an immediate decision that I would stop 50 Division's thrust and throw everything into the outflanking movement, planning to deliver the decisive blow on the El Hamma—Gabes axis before Rommel moved his reserves across to oppose it. I would now endeavour to pin down the Germans in the coastal sector, by giving the impression that I was reorganizing for another attack in that area: meanwhile the western flank would be strongly reinforced. I ordered HQ 10 Corps and 1 Armoured Division to move after dark 23 March to join New Zealand Corps, estimating that they would reach their destination on 25 March. They had to move by the same long and difficult detour as the New Zealanders.

I ordered withdrawal from the north side of the Wall Zigzaou for the night 23/24 March, and this was successfully accomplished under cover of artillery fire.

I also ordered 30 Corps to open up a new thrust in the centre. It seemed clear that 164 Division had moved away from its position at the western end of the Mareth Line proper, and was to oppose the New Zealand Corps in the switch line. There was now, therefore, a good opportunity to open up the road Medenine–Halluf–Bir Soltane through the mountains, which would be an excellent lateral route between my thrust lines, facilitating maintenance and simplifying the switching of forces from one part of the front to another. Moreover, if I could secure the area Toujane-Zelten, and later Matmata, it would be possible to launch 7 Armoured Division through the area to get behind the Mareth positions and cut the Mareth–Gabes road. 4 Indian Division was to undertake this operation and was set in motion after dark 23 March.

As a result of this regrouping, 30 Corps now had on the right 7 Armoured, 50, and 51 Divisions, whose role was to contain the enemy by all possible means, such as raids and artillery fire, to make him prepare for further attacks in the sector. If Rommel did not react to this threat and decided to withdraw troops from the area to reinforce elsewhere, I would be ready to reopen this thrust line. In the centre 4 Indian Division was undertaking a 'short hook' round the Mareth Line, and on the left I had now a very powerful force on El Hamma and Gabes.

My hope was to keep the German reserves involved in the east until my west flank operation got under way. If I could delay the switch of enemy troops for 36 hours, they would be too late to intervene effectively against the outflanking movement. All possible speed was to be employed to mount a 'knock-out' blow by 10 Corps and the New Zealanders, which would burst through the switch line and win the battle.

As HQ 10 Corps (General Horrocks) and 1 Armoured Division were progressing on the long round-about march to join New Zealand Corps, the plan of battle was considered and made ready.

New Zealand Corps was held up at the 'Plum' defile. The Italian troops holding this 6,000 yards bottleneck had been reinforced by Germans, including 21 Panzer Division and 164 Division, and extensive minefields had been laid to strengthen the defences. The enemy had observation over our troops from both sides of the defile, and laborious operations had to be undertaken to secure a foothold on the Djebel Tebaga and on the high ground to the east.

We had now to deliver a lightning attack and break through into the more open country beyond, where the armour would be able to manoeuvre and to continue the offensive to Gabes. The possibility of outflanking the switch line by moving round the western end of the Djebel Tebaga was considered, but I decided against it, since it would have placed a complete obstacle between my forces and rendered mutual support impossible. I considered that the answer was to exploit our great air power, and to subject the enemy to such a weight of concentrated and continuous attack from the air, combined with a full scale land offensive, that he would be unable to withstand the onslaught. The Commander of the Desert Air Force agreed to provide the maximum available degree of intimate co-operation on the battlefield and a joint plan was drawn up.

The basic features of this plan were as follows. The enemy positions were to be heavily bombed throughout the night preceding the attack, so that the defenders would get no sleep and become nervy. The following morning and afternoon bombing would continue, reaching maximum intensity about 1500 hours. Heavy concentrations of artillery would follow for an hour, and the attack would then begin, with the sun behind us. (This was the first occasion in the campaign when we could attack from west to east and so take advantage of the afternoon sun, which in setting would tend to blind the defenders.) The ground attack would aim at pushing the armour through the enemy positions on a very narrow front and orders were given that the advance would continue by moonlight in order to effect the maximum penetration before dawn. To assist the progress of the attack, fighter bombers were to maintain continuous operations by relays of squadrons ahead of the artillery concentrations.

The attack was planned for 1600 hours 26 March.

Meanwhile feints were made on 30 Corps front and 7 Armoured Division was moved up close behind the front line to increase the enemy's anxiety. Air activity was also continued in this sector.

4 Indian Division's attack towards Halluf made good progress and it was reported that the lateral road would soon be open.

26 March dawned with a heavy dust storm blowing, which precluded air attacks during the morning but helped to conceal the forming up of 10 Corps and the New Zealanders. Towards afternoon conditions improved and at 1530 hours the light bombers were over the target area, followed by fighter bombers, which carried out a magnificent operation. For two and a half hours squadrons dropped bombs and shot up enemy troops, transport, and gun positions; they wrought very great moral and material damage on the enemy.

The ground attack started according to plan although the last vehicles of 1 Armoured Division arrived only half an hour before the zero hour, after superhuman efforts had been expended in getting the transport across the difficult country.

With considerable artillery support the New Zealanders (with 8 Armoured Brigade) led the attack, and successfully broke into the enemy defences. 1 Armoured Division followed and penetrated to a depth of 6,000 yards, by which time it was pitch dark and the division was forced to halt. As soon as the moon rose the advance was continued, as it was an essential part of the plan to get through the bottleneck over which the enemy had such excellent observation, before first light. This night advance was a great achievement; in the noise and confusion 1 Armoured Division passed straight through the enemy including the whole of 21 Panzer Division and by dawn on 27 March our leading tanks were only a few miles short of El Hamma where they ran into a strong anti-tank gun screen.

Meanwhile the New Zealand Corps was engaged in very stiff 'mopping up'. The Germans fought savagely and desperately and the task of clearing the battlefield was very severe. But the enemy was in a state of confusion difficult to describe; to the east was 1 Armoured Division and to the west New Zealand Corps, and the enemy was caught between them. Surprise achieved by attacking in the afternoon added to the success, as had the unusual stratagem of driving an armoured formation through the enemy rear areas by moonlight.

Rommel's attempts to reinforce the sector failed. He began to switch his reserves too late, so that they were unable to arrive in time to influence the action. Elements of 15 Panzer Division managed to intervene, but they had no time to deliver any concerted attacks. By evening 27 March the defeat of the enemy had been completed, but not before 21 Panzer Division had made two unsuccessful attacks directed against the rear of 1 Armoured Division.

Meanwhile by midday 27 March, 4 Indian Division had opened the road to Halluf and Bir Soltane, and I had transport made ready for one infantry brigade in case I needed some quick reinforcements in the west.

By night 27/28 March the New Zealand Corps, having completed its operation on the battlefield, was now ready for the next task and was directed on Gabes. We were not successful in cutting off the defenders of the main Mareth

Line, however, as they evacuated their position on the night 27/28 March, and 30 Corps, which began moving after them at first light on 28 March, was confronted with the usual difficulties of mines, booby traps, and demolitions. The same day 10 Corps was delayed in its operations against El Hamma by dust sorms.

SOME REFLECTIONS ON THE BATTLE

The Battle of the Mareth Line was our toughest fight since El Alamein; and whereas the latter was a hard slogging match, at Mareth there had been greater scope for stratagems and subtlety. The defences were exceptionally strong and it was particularly interesting to see how well the covering positions had been sited in order to mislead the attacker in his efforts to contact the main position. The prelude to our victory had been the Battle of Medenine on 6 March; Rommel's abortive attack had failed to interrupt our preparations, and served only to increase the morale of the Eighth Army. The fifty-two tanks which the enemy lost there must have been sorely missed at the switch line on 26 and 27 March! As at El Alamein, Rommel cast in his reserves piecemeal, and when the battle started his armour was spreadeagled—with 10 Panzer Division in the Gafsa sector, 15 Panzer Division soon involved on the coast, and 21 Panzer Division arriving in the west to back up the switch line.

The outstanding feature of the battle was the air action in co-operation with the outflanking forces. Several new methods of controlling aircraft working over the battlefield were tried out on this occasion; a Royal Air Force officer observed the battle from a forward observation post, in order to give the pilots (by direct radio link) information about the enemy and our own troops. Our air superiority was virtually complete, and we were never bothered by enemy air action.

We retained the initiative throughout. Even when we lost our gains on the coastal flank, Rommel was kept on the move by the speedy development of the western outflanking movement; having stopped the thrust on the coast, he was not able to switch troops to the El Hamma sector in time to hold us there. The most crucial time in this battle was in the early hours of 23 March, when I made an immediate decision at 0200 hours to switch the whole weight of the attack to the extreme west, discontinuing meanwhile efforts on the coastal axis. Following this decision, the vital considerations were, first, the speed with which the decisive blow could be mounted and delivered and, secondly, the necessity to hold the German reserves on the eastern flank long enough to prevent their assisting the defenders of the switch line west of El Hamma.

As a result of the battle, 15 and 21 Panzer Divisions received a tremendous hammering and 164 Division lost most of its heavy weapons and vehicles. At least three Italian Divisions lost so many prisoners that they were of little fighting value in the future. 2,500 prisoners, mostly Germans, were taken at El Hamma and up to 28 March the total for the battle was 7,000.

CHAPTER EIGHT

THE BATTLE OF WADI AKARIT (6 APRIL 1943) AND THE ADVANCE TO ENFIDAVILLE

SITUATION AFTER THE BATTLE OF THE MARETH LINE

To the immediate north of the Mareth Line the coastal plain widens between Gabes and El Hamma, but beyond the main road between those places a serious bottleneck is reached, known to us at the time as the Gabes Gap. The gap extends from the coast to the eastern extremity of the system of lakes and marshes called locally Shott el Fejaj and is some 12 to 15 miles wide. Across the gap, a little to the north of its narrowest part, runs the Wadi Akarit, a difficult obstacle to the movement of tanks and vehicles. The north bank of the wadi is dominated by a line of steep sided hills, the main features on the coastal sector being Djebel er Roumana, which extends to within a few miles of the sea, and Djebel Fatnassa.

The Wadi Akarit thus formed an extremely strong natural defensive position and it was to be expected that the enemy would make use of it; in fact, I had always had this possibility in mind when considering the problem of getting to Sfax.

When Rommel evacuated the Mareth defences he gathered his forces for the defence of the Gabes Gap. As usual he held his front chiefly with Italians and his main reserves were 15 Panzer Division and 90 Light Division. My problem was to prevent his settling into this new position and to burst though the gap myself as quickly as possible.

It will be recalled that on 28 March 10 Corps was ordered to send the New Zealanders direct to Gabes and to capture El Hamma. The task of 30 Corps was to advance on

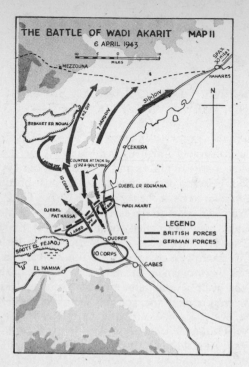

THE BATTLE OF WADI AKARIT   MAP II
6 APRIL 1943

the axis of the main Mareth–Gabes road.

On 29 March the enemy withdrew under pressure from El Hamma and 1 Armoured Division was soon north of the town. On the same day Gabes and Oudref fell to the New Zealanders. Contact was now established with the enemy on the line of the Wadi Akarit with the New Zealanders on the right and 1 Armoured Division on the left. 30 Corps was positioned in rear, between Mareth and Gabes. As we probed the new enemy position, it became clear that Rommel was going to attempt a firm stand—an inevitable decision—as he needed time to reorganize his forces after the defeat he had just sustained.

On 30 March I ordered 10 Corps to get close contact

with the Akarit defences and to determine whether they could be forced by the Corps with its existing resources. 30 Corps meanwhile was to prepare to deliver a staged attack to gain a bridgehead, in case 10 Corps found the opposition to be very strong. I now abolished the temporary New Zealand Corps, for it had served its purpose admirably and was no longer required.

The next day 10 Corps reported to me that the wadi could be forced by the New Zealand Division but that the operation would probably involve considerable casualties. I did not want to risk this, since the division would be invaluable for the mobile phase which lay ahead. I therefore decided to regroup. 30 Corps took over temporary command of 2 New Zealand Division and also responsibility for the front. It would carry out the attack on the Akarit position with 4 Indian and 51 Divisions, in order to secure a bridgehead through which 10 Corps would pass. 10 Corps taking with it the New Zealanders, would be direct on the Mezzouna group of airfields. 30 Corps would advance on the coast road axis to Mahares on a narrow front using 51 Division only; as soon as there was room to manoeuvre, 7 Armoured Division would be released for operations to the west of the coast road.

I subsequently decided to increase the assaulting force available for the coming battle; 30 Corps was now to assault with 51, 50, and 4 Indian Divisions, keeping 2 New Zealand Division in a holding role on the front. This was necessary because the strength of the opposition was greater than I at first imagined. The enemy had complete observation over us and the task ahead was formidable. Energetic measures were taken to improve our tank strength, ready for the mobile warfare which was to come, and by 4 April I had nearly 500 tanks available (including the seventy Valentines of 23 Armoured Brigade).

The battle began at 0400 hours 6 April in the dark. Previously our night attacks had always been mounted in moonlight, but I could not wait ten days for the next moon and so decided to change the technique and to attack in the dark; I hoped to gain surprise in this way and indeed was successful. Objectives on the right (51 Division) and left (4 Indian Division) were quickly gained, but 50 Division in the centre had difficulty in the wadi and was delayed until the middle of the day.

The Germans were determined to hold us back and the fighting was bitter. Heavy and determined counter attacks were staged by 15 Panzer and 90 Light Divisions and some localities changed hands several times. My troops fought magnificently, particularly 51 and 4 Indian Divisions, and hung on to the key localities they had taken. The enemy knew that if I could now bring 10 Corps through into the open, he was finished; if I forced him to withdraw he would have no alternative but to go back to the high ground north of Enfidaville: sacrificing the maritime plain and the ports of Sfax and Sousse.

My object was to maintain the momentum of attack. As long as this was done the enemy would be unable to recover, and my superior resources would enable me to continue the pressure until he cracked. I ordered 10 Corps to smash its way out through the front. By noon 6 April it was on the move, headed by 2 New Zealand Division which I had reverted to 10 Corps for the purpose.

By immense endeavours, however, the enemy prevented me from breaking out into the open before dark. But he had exhausted himself; meanwhile I was ready to stage a major 'break-out' action with full scale air and artillery support on 7 April.

Rommel did not wait for the blow to fall but pulled back during the night 6/7 April, and by dawn was in full retreat. The pursuit was taken up according to plan, with 30 Corps on the coastal axis and 10 Corps inland.

Over 7,000 prisoners (mostly Italian), were taken in the battle, and once again Rommel had been defeated and thrown back to the north. He had been surprised by our attack in the darkness, and his troops were overwhelmed by the violence of the 'break-in' operation and by the sustained pressure which followed it.

By the evening of 7 April, leading troops were on the general line Cekhira–Sebkret er Noual. The countryside was littered with burning vehicles and abandoned equipment, and everywhere parties of Italians were encountered, wandering southwards to give themselves into captivity. On the coastal axis 15 Panzer and 90 Light Divisions provided the enemy rearguards, and intense fighting continued in some areas.

Meanwhile 2 United States Corps in the Gafsa sector was on the move again and on 7 April contact was made between that formation and forward elements of 10 Corps on the Gabes–Gafsa road.

Further north 9 Corps of First Army had started an offensive at the Fondouk Gap and on 9 April, 6 Armoured Division broke through to the east directed on Kairouan.

On 9 April, 30 Corps continued to meet stubborn resistance from enemy rearguards but maintained steady pressure. At last light 22 Armoured Brigade (7 Armoured Division) was but only a few miles short of Sfax, having had a most successful engagement near Agareb against 15 Panzer Division which had been caught ambushed on the move. 10 Corps forged ahead and was directed now on the airfields at Triaga and Fauconnerie. I ordered it subsequently to swing towards the coast at La Hencha to loosen the opposition to 30 Corps.

Sfax was captured on the morning of 10 April. Incidentally, back in Tripoli, I had been promised a Flying Fortress for my own use if I captured Sfax by 15 April. This was soon afterwards generously sent to me by General Eisenhower and for the remainder of the war I had an American aircraft at my disposal.

2 New Zealand Division reached La Hencha and the drive northwards continued. The administrative situation

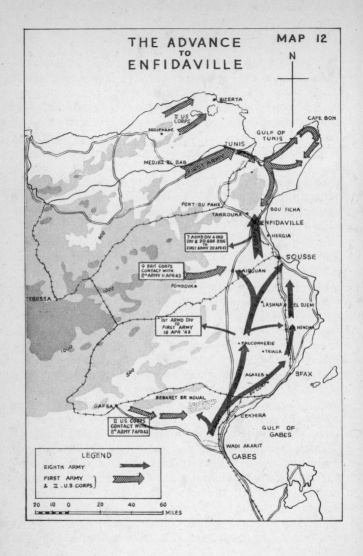

THE ADVANCE TO ENFIDAVILLE

MAP 12

N

BIZERTA

II US CORPS

SEDJENANE

CAPE BON

GULF OF TUNIS

TUNIS

MEDJEZ EL BAB

PONT DU FAHS

BOU FICHA

TAKROUNA

ENFIDAVILLE

HERGLA

7 ARMD DIV 4 IND DIV & 20 GDS BDE TO FIRST ARMY 30 APR 43

SOUSSE

9 BRIT CORPS CONTACT WITH 8TH ARMY 8 APR 43

KAIROUAN

FONDOUK

LASHALA

EL DJEM

TEBESSA

1st ARMD DIV TO FIRST ARMY 18 APR '43

LA HENCHA

FAUCONNERIE

TRIAGA

AGAREB

SFAX

SEBKRET ER NOUAL

II US CORPS CONTACT WITH 8TH ARMY 7 APR 43

GAFSA

CEKHIRA

GULF OF GABES

WADI AKARIT

GABES

LEGEND

EIGHTH ARMY

FIRST ARMY & II. U.S. CORPS

20 10 0   20   40   60
MILES

again needed careful watching, as I was still maintaining the army along the single road from Tripoli—now some 300 miles away. It became urgent to get the port of Sfax working.

My orders on 11 April to 10 Corps were to capture Sousse and to join up with First Army at Kairouan, as 6 Armoured Division was now in that area. 1 Armoured Division was halted in the Fauconnerie area. 30 Corps was instructed to move 4 Indian and 50 Divisions north from the Akarit position to join 10 Corps. I decided to hold in reserve Headquarters 30 Corps, with 7 Armoured and 51 Divisions, about Sfax.

Sousse fell on 12 April and by the end of the following day the leading troops of 10 Corps were up against the anti-tank ditch at Enfidaville. Meanwhile we were receiving reports about the enemy positions constructed along the high ground which forms the northern barrier of the maritime plain and reaches almost to the sea just north of Enfidaville. This defensive system became known to Eighth Army as the Enfidaville position.

The Allies were closing in on the Axis forces, and it was now appreciated that the enemy intended to stand on the line Enfidaville–Pont du Fahs–Medjez el Bab–Sedjenane. On 12 April I received word from General Alexander that First Army was to make the main effort in the final phase of the North African Campaign, and that Eighth Army's role would be to exert the maximum pressure on the southern sector of the enemy's front in order to pin down as much of his strength as possible. The plain west of Tunis was the most suitable ground for the deployment of armoured forces and I was asked to send an armoured division and an armoured car regiment to join First Army.

I nominated 1 Armoured Division and the King's Dragoon Guards for this role and in due course they joined 9 Corps.

The Enfidaville position was admirably suited for defence and unless the enemy could be 'bounced' out of it before he had time to organize his defences thoroughly, it was obviously going to be a very difficult undertaking to break through it. The country was generally unsuitable for tanks, except in the very narrow coastal strip, and even there water channels and other obstacles existed. The enemy had excellent observation over our territory to the south; moreover he showed every indication of being prepared to stand and put up a desperate fight.

In these circumstances the decision that the main effort should now be transferred to the Plain of Tunis was a logical one.

I gave orders for 'squaring up' to the Enfidaville position. 10 Corps (now consisting of 7 Armoured, 2 New Zealand, 4 Indian, and 50 Divisions) was instructed to endeavour to push the enemy out of the position before he had settled in. The attempt would be made on the coastal axis, and if successful 10 Corps would go on to the next system of defences which were known to exist about Bou-Ficha. If the enemy could not be 'bounced' out, I planned to stage a full scale thrust on the night of 19/20 April.

I intended to retain Headquarters 30 Corps and 51 Division in reserve.

The Desert Air Force meanwhile 'stepped up' to landing grounds in the area Sousse–El Djem–La Smala–Kairouan. This was destined to be its last move in the campaign, since from these fields it could operate throughout the zone remaining to the enemy in Tunisia.

I had from this time to take into account the future role of the Eighth Army when deciding on the grouping and tasks of the various divisions. I had been told in January, when at Tripoli, that the Eighth Army was to form the Imperial component of the combined British and American force destined to invade Sicily, as soon as practicable after the completion of the campaign in North Africa. I was anxious to rest Headquarters 30 Corps and get it prepared for starting on the new task; I should also require 51 Division and either 2 New Zealand or 50 Division for the assault on

Sicily, and these formations would have to be refitted and rested before beginning this new enterprise.

By 16 April it was plain that the enemy could not be 'bounced' out of his new defence system and I ordered preparations to be made for a heavy attack using 2 New Zealand and 4 Indian Divisions for the main thrust astride the village of Takrouna, 50 Division for a subsidiary blow on the coast road axis, and 7 Armoured Division for guarding the western flank, linking up on its left with the French 19 Corps.

I called forward 56 Division from Tripoli so that I could relieve 2 New Zealand or 50 Division when the time came for the formation selected to return to Egypt for reorganization.

THE BATTLE OF ENFIDAVILLE

On the night 19/20 April the attack against the Enfidaville position began. A great weight of artillery support was provided and the customary air programme arranged.

It was quickly apparent that we were going to have difficulty in this task. We were hurling ourselves against a formidable barrier of difficult ground and the defenders were strengthened in their endeavours by the desperate necessity of holding their remaining bridgehead in Africa. Fighting was severe, particularly in Takrouna, but the New Zealanders captured the vital ground we needed. On the right Enfidaville fell and we pushed forward some three miles beyond, while on the left we secured the ground necessary to deny the enemy observation over areas required for the forward deployment of artillery. A series of heavy counter attacks was staged by the enemy on 20 and 21 April, but we retained a firm grip on our gains and advanced another three miles along the coast. The Germans suffered heavy casualties and 800 prisoners were taken in the first two days.

I decided that it was too expensive to continue the thrust

in the centre and on 22 April ordered regrouping of the Army, in order to switch the main thrust line to the coast. At the same time I had to relieve 50 Division, which was now to return to Egypt to prepare for Sicily.

The regrouping went ahead, but the more I examined the problem now confronting Eighth Army, the more convinced I became that our operations would be extremely costly and had little chance of achieving any decisive success with the resources available. The enemy was located in ideal defensive country and could find a series of excellent positions, one behind the other, from which to oppose us and there was no scope for deploying my armour.

THE END OF THE NORTH AFRICAN CAMPAIGN

On 30 April General Alexander visited me and we discussed the whole problem of finishing the war in North Africa. Subsequently a major regrouping between First and Eighth Armies was ordered, with the object of strengthening the projected thrust across the Plain of Tunis to the sea. 7 Armoured and 4 Indian Divisions, 201 Guards Brigade, and some medium artillery were switched to First Army and General Horrocks went to command 9 Corps, whose Commander had been wounded.

I was left with 2 New Zealand, 51 and 56 Divisions, a French Division now placed under my command, and two armoured brigades. I decided to hold the front with 56 and 12 French Divisions, to keep 51 Division in reserve (where it might commence training for Sicily) and to employ 2 New Zealand Division with an armoured brigade for an operation on the western flank towards Saouf.

Meanwhile on 6 May First Army launched an attack in great strength from the Medjez el Bab sector, directed on Tunis. Complete success was achieved, and both Tunis and Bizerta fell on 7 May. I was happy to learn that 7 Armoured Division was first into Tunis. Mopping up of the enemy forces continued until 12 May, when the last resistance ceased.

The North Africa Campaign had reached its conclusion and the remaining Axis survivors were lodged in captivity. It had ended in a major disaster for the Germans; all their remaining troops, equipment, and stores were captured. Very few personnel were able to get away owing to the effectiveness of the blockade by the Royal Navy and Royal Air Force which closed the escape routes by sea and air. It is idle to speculate why the Axis forces attempted to hold on in North Africa once the Mareth Line and Gabes Gap had been forced. From a purely military point of view there was no justification for their action, but perhaps there were overriding political considerations.

The Eighth Army had travelled 1,850 miles from El Alamein to be in at the death and was now destined to have a short respite. Within two months it was taking part in the opening stage of the first entry into Hitler's 'Fortress of Europe'.

Headquarters and some of the divisions of Eighth Army moved back to the Tripoli area as soon as their task in Tunisia was completed and, before starting on the next enterprise, were honoured by a visit from His Majesty The King—a fitting climax to our campaigning in Africa.

CHAPTER NINE

ADMINISTRATION IN THE NORTH AFRICAN CAMPAIGN

When I took over command of the Eighth Army both the staffs of the formations and the troops themselves had already acquired a considerable degree of skill in the rather specialized form of administration necessary in desert warfare. They had learned in the hard school of experience. Two rapid advances to the El Agheila position, succeeded by desperate withdrawals, had led to drastic modifications in previously accepted methods and to the establishment of new procedures for dealing with the conditions obtaining in the desert.

One principle of great value and importance had already been fully accepted, namely that the Staff must exercise a firm control over the administrative plan and watchful co-ordination over its execution. The day had gone when the Head of a Service could say 'The efficiency of my Service is my own concern. Tell me what you want me to do and leave me alone to do it.' It had also been realized that the various administrative installations which are set up to support a formation in battle need centralized control. The Field Maintenance Centre, a sort of administrative township with a headquarters to control it, comprised those installations which were necessary for the support of a Corps. This first made its appearance in the offensive of November 1941 and was by now an established element of administrative organization. The Army Roadhead, which first came into being as such during the Alamein Campaign, was but a development of the same idea.

The Field Maintenance Centre and Army Roadhead represented a departure from previous practice, not only by virtue of their own organization but even more importantly because of the stocks which they held. All textbooks written before the War had assumed that requirements of a force would be met by the despatch of daily pack trains. It was considered neither necessary nor desirable to hold any reserves at a railhead, or forward of it, except in very small amounts necessary to balance deliveries. The campaigns of 1940 and 1941 had shown that this system was not workable in modern conditions of warfare. It was too inflexible. During a rapid advance the demand for petrol rose to staggering levels. By the time that the necessary adjustments had been made in pack train loadings, the need for the petrol had given way to a demand for ammunition because the advance had been stopped and battle was imminent. It is of course true that the holding of large supplies well forward had disadvantages. In spite of every effort made for their destruction, considerable supplies fell into the enemy's hands during the retreat from Gazala to Alamein. As a result of this misfortune an attempt was made to adopt once again the pack train system during the period of static warfare on the Alamein position. The attempt had to be abandoned immediately the advance began. The upshot of this matter is that, if a commander loses his battle, his defeat will be the more serious if he had held reserves forward which fall into the enemy's hands. On the other hand, if he wins his battle, he will not be able to take advantage of victory unless he has such reserves. I have always planned on the assumption of success.

Another lesson which had already been well learnt was the importance of the recovery of armoured vehicles and M.T. The arrangements for this had been brought to a state of efficiency which stood us in excellent stead throughout the advance.

The set-piece battle of Alam Halfa and Alamein presented no unusual or particularly difficult administrative problems. The Army was close to its base, to which it was linked both by rail and road. The pursuit from Alamein to Tripoli and

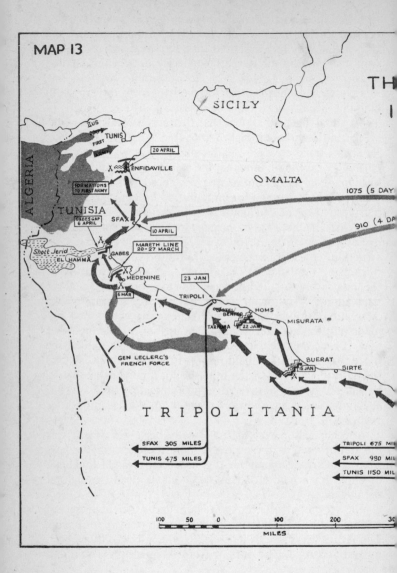

MAP 13

TH

SICILY

ALGERIA

TUNIS

FIRST

FIRST ARMY

20 APRIL

ENFIDAVILLE

MALTA

1075 (5 DAY

FORMATIONS
TO FIRST ARMY

TUNISIA

GABES GAP
6 APRIL

SFAX

910 (4 DA

10 APRIL

Shott Jerid

EL HAMMA

GABES

MARETH LINE
20-27 MARCH

MEDENINE

23 JAN

TRIPOLI

5 MAR

HOMS

CASTEL
BENITO

MISURATA

TARHUNA

22 JAN

GEN LECLERC'S
FRENCH FORCE

BUERAT

15 JAN

SIRTE

T R I P O L I T A N I A

SFAX   305 MILES

TUNIS 475 MILES

TRIPOLI 675 MIL

SFAX   980 MIL

TUNIS 1150 MIL

100   50   0   100   200   30

MILES

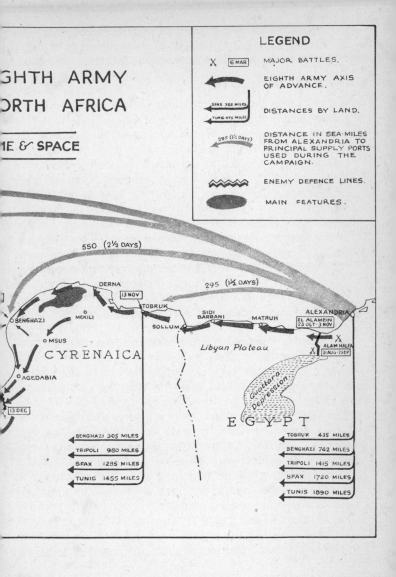

EIGHTH ARMY
NORTH AFRICA

TIME & SPACE

550 (2½ DAYS)

295 (1½ DAYS)

DERNA

13 NOV

TOBRUK

SIDI
BARRANI   MATRUH

ALEXANDRIA

EL ALAMEIN
23 OCT - 3 NOV

BENGHAZI   MEKILI

SOLLUM

X

X   ALAM HALFA
31 AUG - 7 SEP

MSUS

CYRENAICA

Libyan Plateau

Quattara
Depression

AGEDABIA

13 DEC

E G Y P T

BENGHAZI 305 MILES
TRIPOLI 980 MILES
SFAX 1285 MILES
TUNIS 1455 MILES

TOBRUK 435 MILES
BENGHAZI 742 MILES
TRIPOLI 1415 MILES
SFAX 1720 MILES
TUNIS 1890 MILES

from Tripoli to Tunis, may, on the other hand, be regarded as an administrative campaign of unprecedented interest. It is possible here only to mention some of its outstanding features. Those who are interested in the study of administration in modern warfare should make a detailed examination of it.

I must first pay tribute to those who were responsible for administrative planning at GHQ Middle East Forces. The build-up of the fighting troops which enabled me to win the victory of El Alamein would have been of no avail unless it had been accompanied by an intelligent reinforcement on a large scale of our administrative resources. It would have been of no avail because I should have been unable to reap the fruits of victory. It was a good example of the foresight which is the essence of a successful administration in war.

The keynote of my administrative arrangements throughout the pursuit was austerity. Even with the generous resources provided, the task of administration was immense. Administrative considerations dictated, throughout, the strength of the force which could be deployed at any given time. It follows from this that everything which accompanied the leading troops had to be very carefully scrutinized. We could afford no luxuries. To carry forward more equipment or more men than were absolutely necessary for the battle meant a subtraction from our fighting strength. It was equally essential that the administrative organization itself should be pruned to the limit. In order that it may do itself justice, there is always a tendency for an administrative service to provide for all contingencies. This we could not afford. I must mention particularly the use of fighting troops for work on essential administrative tasks. Infantry were used to help in the discharge of ships at Benghazi, Tripoli and at the small coves between these two places where we landed supplies from craft. By using reserve formations for this purpose we avoided the necessity of bringing forward a corresponding number of pioneer companies. It is most important in such circumstances to explain both to officers and men why they are being used for a task for which otherwise they would have little relish. They must not become discouraged and lose efficiency. The scale of reserves was kept to a minimum throughout, with the result that on isolated occasions certain units were short. This is inevitable in such conditions. If *all* troops had had *all* that they needed *all* the time, it would have been proof that administration had over-insured. In particular the amount of ammunition allowed for each battle was calculated to a nicety with the result that when the action had been fought very little remained on the ground. I think it most important to emphasize this matter of austerity because in subsequent campaigns, when conditions were entirely different, we were able to be more lavish and our troops became accustomed to having everything of which they felt a need. If the British Army has to fight another war, I feel sure that at the outset it will have to operate under an austere regime of administration and not under the relatively comfortable conditions which obtained during the latter phase of this War.

A feature of our administrative arrangements during this campaign, which may fairly be regarded as new, was the organization of what may be termed the 'administrative assault force'. While preparations for the attack at Alamein were being made there was being formed simultaneously a force of administrative units drawn from all three Services. A Commander and staff were appointed to co-ordinate their movements and activities. The role of this force was to advance close on the heels of the fighting troops and to take over as quickly as possible ports and other places of administrative importance and to organize them rapidly for the reception and distribution of supplies. Several references have been made in previous chapters to the work done in opening and developing harbours. This is a combined operation in which all three Services play an essential part and must work together. The three most important members of the administrative assault force were the Area Commander, the Naval Officer in Charge and the Air Officer responsible for fighter defence. These three with their staffs and services lived together during the planning stage and moved forward together on a co-ordinated plan. Special priority tables were worked out to ensure that they should get forward and reach their objective at the earliest possible moment. The name 'Golden List' was applied to these tables and remained in use in subsequent campaigns. The position of each unit on the 'Golden List' was very carefully worked out by the administrative staff. It is possible to keep the same administrative assault force in the van throughout the advance. Alternatively, more than one such force can be organized and the leap-frog principle adopted. The former system, by producing a team of very highly trained and experienced men, ensures that the organization of administration at the most forward point is carried out as rapidly as possible. On the other hand, due to the fact that the spearhead is constantly on the move, the organization of the port or administrative area suffers more at a later stage and the leap-frog principle has an advantage in this respect.

From Alamein to Tunis the advance of the Eighth Army was carried out by well defined bounds. There is always a tendency, natural and indeed laudable, on the part of keen commanders to edge forward as far as possible at all times. When administration is strained this tendency must be checked; it prevents the accumulation of reserves and this means that the mounting of a powerful attack becomes impossible.

The problem of the division of administrative control first came into prominence during this campaign. During the early stage of the advance, the administrative staff of Eighth Army had control of the railhead or port on which the Army was mainly based and of the entire area in front of it. GHQ Middle East Forces assumed control progressively in rear. Rear Army Headquarters had necessarily to be located near the main railhead or port. This meant a separation in distance which sometimes exceeded 200 miles between Rear Army Headquarters and Main Army Headquarters, at

106

which latter place the chief administrative officer was located. When we reached Tripoli I felt that some alteration in this arrangement was necessary. GHQ Middle East Forces could not assume responsibility for Tripoli because it was too far away and there was no communication other than wireless. Moreover, it was undesirable that it should do so because of the vital dependence of my operational plans on the functioning of the port and its depots. To meet this situation I organized a special staff under a Major-General which not only took charge of the local administration of the Tripoli Area, but, working in very close contact with the Army staff, also became responsible for the formulation of demands on GHQ Middle East Forces. This was the first attempt to solve a problem which repeated itself in Sicily and Italy.

PART TWO

THE INVASION AND CAPTURE OF SICILY
10 JULY–17 AUGUST 1943

CHAPTER TEN

PLANNING THE INVASION OF SICILY

THE EVOLUTION OF THE PLAN

As the first stage in the policy of striking at the 'underbelly' of Axis Europe, the British and American Governments authorized the invasion of Sicily. The operation was to follow the North African campaign as quickly as conditions permitted, and it was decided that both United States and Empire troops, under the supreme command of General Eisenhower, would take part.

Under the Supreme Commander the Service chiefs appointed were Admiral Cunningham, General Alexander and Air Marshal Tedder. The forces were to be organized in two commands, the Western (United States) and Eastern (British) Naval and Military Task Forces; Allied air resources remained centralized. The Eighth Army formed the military component of the Eastern Task Force, in which my Service colleagues were Admiral Ramsay and Air Vice-Marshal Park (later Air Vice-Marshal Broadhurst).

Late in January 1943, orders to plan and mount Operation 'Husky', as the invasion was called, were received in North Africa, and a planning staff (initially known as Force 141 and later expanded on the Army side into HQ 15 Army Group) was set up in Algiers to commence work on the problem.

It will be noticed that at this time the Tunisian campaign had not yet entered into its last phases. Eighth Army had recently captured Tripoli and First Army was operating in the mountains of western Tunisia, so that the commanders and troops destined to undertake this great combined operation were fully committed in the immediate battle. As a result there were serious delays in planning 'Husky' and in fact the preparation of the expedition was beset with tremendous difficulties at all levels of command throughout the period available for the task.

Before dealing with the development of detailed planning in the Eastern Task Force, I will discuss the evolution of the plan of invasion, for this was a matter which took considerable time and was brought to finality only after much discussion and delay.

Although I knew in January that Eighth Army was to take part in 'Husky', it was not until 23 April that I had an opportunity of leaving the battle in Tunisia for a few days (while my formations were regrouping before Enfidaville) in order to make a detailed study of the proposed outline plan. The original version had been produced by joint Allied planning staffs and with certain modifications was under discussion at Force 141. A series of planning staffs was concerned with the examination of the plan, but had to function without the customary and essential guidance of the commanders directly responsible for carrying out the operation. This system of 'absentee landlords' led to all the obvious disadvantages.

After examination I came to the conclusion that the existing plan was unsound, and immediately submitted my views to General Alexander. The plan proposed was that Sicily should be invaded simultaneously in two distinct areas: by the Western Task Force in the north-west corner of the island, and by the Eastern Task Force in the south-east on a frontage between the Gulf of Catania and the Gulf of Gela. For the assault the Americans were to have shipping and craft for three divisions with some armoured troops, with another equivalent division available to discharge immediately behind the assault; Eighth Army would have four assaulting divisions, with a tank brigade in 'floating reserve'. An airborne division was available for each task force.

The most important immediate objectives were ports and airfields. Ports were essential quickly as there was no available experience of maintenance over beaches, which was viewed with the greatest mistrust. The distance of Sicily from our available airfields made it essential, moreover, to establish the air forces in the island urgently, or the Axis air force would be able to interfere with our landings and sea routes, perhaps with disastrous results. These considerations were covered by the proposed plan, which provided (in the case of the Eastern Task Force) for the early capture of two groups of airfields (the Catania group and the Comiso—Gela group) and the ports in the south-east of the island—Catania, Augusta and Siracusa.

But—and to my mind this was the vital point—the proposed plan was based on the existing enemy garrison in Sicily in early 1943 and assumed that the Axis powers would not reinforce the island before our invasion. To spread four divisions, with a relatively slow build-up of forces behind them, between the Gulf of Catania and Gela obviously implied negligible resistance to our assault and a decision on the part of the enemy not to send reinforcements from Italy to oppose us.

I had seen the fierce resistance that the Germans and Italians were showing in Tunisia and considered that it was essential to prepare to meet strong enemy reaction in Sicily. By the time we launched the invasion there was no reason to suppose that the island garrison would not be reinforced; moreover the Axis powers could send troops across the Straits of Messina more quickly than we could hope to build up our forces across the sea. To assume negligible resistance to our enterprise and to disperse our assaulting divisions, therefore, appeared to me fundamentally unsound and the first point upon which I made strong representations was that the formations of the Eastern Task Force must land within supporting distance of each other. A suitable area could then be secured as a firm base from which to develop further operations. This conclusion led me to propose an alternative plan.

The essentials of the problem from the Army's point of view were that a bridgehead had to be seized, the choice of which was limited to those areas of the island which were within fighter range of our aerodromes; its size was dependent on the available forces, which had to be landed concentrated and prepared for hard fighting. Within the bridgehead it was essential to secure the port and airfield facilities without which the combined operation would inevitably collapse. Applied to 'Husky', these factors led to the conclusion that the best area for putting the Eighth Army ashore was in the Gulf of Noto and astride the Pachino peninsula. This would limit the frontage of assault to suit our resources and a suitable firm base could be developed from the beaches across the south-east portion of the island; Siracusa could be captured rapidly and operations swung northwards to secure Augusta and Catania. But this possibility did not satisfy one essential requirement: the seizure of an adequate number of airfields. The air forces were insistent that the Comiso—Gela group must be included in the initial bridgehead: not only in order to deny the fields to the enemy, but also to enable our own squadrons to deploy in sufficient strength to dominate the enemy air force and assist in the development of our operations.

Here then was an impasse, nor was there an alternative area of assault for the Eastern Task Force which could satisfy the demands of all three Services. If the proposed bridgehead were shifted north to include Catania and its airfields, we should overshoot the zone of fighter cover; if moved westwards to include Comiso and Gela there was no immediate prospect of capturing ports: and with its existing resources the Army was unable to accept the degree of dispersion which would embrace both the ports and airfields required.

I therefore recommended that the Eastern Task Force should be allotted two more assaulting divisions, with adequate build-up resources, to enable us to assault on a frontage from the Gulf of Noto to Gela inclusive.

On 2 May I attended a conference at Algiers and put forward my views. The outcome was a decision by the

Supreme Commander to shift the assault of the American Seventh Army from the north-west corner of the island to the Gulf of Gela. This implied that the two task forces would land side by side within mutual supporting distance and would secure a bridgehead which included all the vital requirements of the Navy, and Air Forces. I heard of General Eisenhower's decision on 3 May and from that date detailed planning was able to progress on a firm basis.

I based my outline plan on having available 10, 13, and 30 Corps. Briefly my intention was as follows:

13 Corps would land in the Gulf of Noto south of Siracusa with two divisions. Its task would be to secure the high ground overlooking the beaches, then wheel north to capture successively Siracusa, Augusta, and Catania. The Corps would be assisted by a seaborne commando operation and by airborne landings. Astride the Pachino peninsula 30 Corps would assault with two divisions and secure a firm base from which it would join up with the American forces to the north-west, and operate to the north in order to take over the 13 Corps beachhead. In this way units of 13 Corps would be released for the capture of Siracusa and the other ports.

I decided to hold 10 Corps in reserve in the Tripoli area.

SOME PLANNING DIFFICULTIES CONFRONTING THE EASTERN TASK FORCE

I have mentioned that the preparations for this operation were carried out in extremely difficult conditions. The Eastern Task Force planning headquarters was in Cairo. In April I started sending members of Eighth Army staff from Tunisia to Cairo and gradually assembled there a nucleus from the various branches. Not until 16 May was HQ Eighth Army proper released from Tunisia.

Releasing troops from the battle in order that they could reorganize and commence training for combined operations had proved very difficult, but it will be recalled that I had kept HQ 30 Corps and 51 Division in reserve during the

115

final phase in Tunisia and that 50 Division had been relieved by 56 Division before the end of the North African campaign. Meanwhile HQ 13 Corps (General Dempsey) was in the Delta, having been out of the line since El Alamein.

Thus it will be evident that circumstances prevented a 'tidy' start being made on preparations for the 'Husky' venture.

The mounting of the Eastern Task Force was primarily the responsibility of GHQ Middle East, but part of the force was mounted in Tunisia and one division in England. The detailed planning was done by Task Force Headquarters and 13 Corps in Cairo; 30 Corps completed its planning in Tunisia; 10 Corps was at Tripoli; and our immediate superior headquarters was at Algiers.

The troops destined to take part were even more dispersed. 1 Canadian Division, located in England, was to join the assault direct from home ports. 51 and 78 Divisions were to embark in Tunisia, where 1 Airborne Division was based inland at Kairouan. In the Tripoli area I had 7 Armoured and 56 Divisions. In the Middle East, destined to embark at Alexandria, the Canal ports and at Haifa were 5 and 50 Divisions together with 231 Infantry Brigade (which had formerly been in Malta).

The detailed order of battle was a nightmare because it was not known until the end of the North African campaign which divisions would in fact emerge in sufficient strength and condition to be ready for Sicily in the time available. The planning of the assault was subject to the availability of various types of assault craft and ships, a factor which constantly changed up to the very last minute: with the inevitable repercussions on the planning of the units and formations concerned. Not the least of the difficulties arose from relatively minor matters such as the difference between the War Establishment tables in England, the Middle East and North Africa, which resulted in seemingly endless misunderstandings, when staff work was being handled over such immense distances.

In the wider aspect of planning for the whole Task Force, the main difficulty was the separation of the Navy and Army staffs from their Air Force counterpart. The air forces were represented in Cairo by a liaison staff provided from North Africa, but the Air Force Command immediately concerned with our activities was in Malta: very busily involved with air operations for which Malta was a key base. It was therefore impossible to plan in close contact with the actual air staff with which the battle was to be conducted at the Task Force level. A further complication which affected the Army was that as soon as units of our tactical air component were established in Sicily, they were to come under command of a different Air Force headquarters.

Between the Royal Navy and the Army there were no such complications, for the two staffs worked together in close harmony in the same building in Cairo.

During the preparatory period formations and units carried out intensive training and special courses were arranged at the available Combined Operations centres. Formations reorganized, absorbed their quotas of reinforcements and were re-equipped while staffs worked feverishly at the mass of detailed preparation which an invasion demands. Perhaps the most difficult problem which faced the subordinate formations of the Army arose from continually varying estimates of availability of craft and shipping. For example, every time an assault craft is added to, or still worse, subtracted from, the allotment made to a unit, the leading tables and probably the detailed tactical plan have to be revised, and the alteration may have repercussions on the next higher formation as well as on subordinate sub-units. Moreover, the availability of the various types of special assault craft was very limited, so that the scope for organization of assaulting units and tactical grouping in craft was greatly restricted. Yet another complication was the time which units and formations would be at sea before the landing operation began; troops cannot be packed into landing craft for long periods, when such craft are designed to

117

carry them relatively short distances.

I will not elaborate on these difficulties, for I have given sufficient instances to make it clear that the planning and mounting of Operation 'Husky' presented a formidable task.

<h2 style="text-align:center">THE OVERALL PLAN</h2>

During May and June the detailed plan took shape. The Supreme Commander's orders gave as his intention the seizure of Sicily. The operation was to be conducted in five phases; first, the preparatory measures by Naval and Air Forces to neutralize enemy naval efforts and to gain air supremacy; second, the seaborne assault, assisted by airborne landings, with the object of seizing airfields and the ports of Siracusa and Licata; third, the establishment of a firm base from which to conduct operations for the capture of the ports of Augusta and Catania and the airfields in the Plain of Catania; fourth, the capture of these ports and airfields; finally, the reduction of the island.

Eighth Army's task was to assault between Siracusa and Pozzallo to capture the port of Siracusa and the airfield at Pachino. We were then to advance to the general line Siracusa–Palazzolo–Ragusa, making contact at Ragusa with Seventh United States Army. Subsequently we were to secure Augusta and Catania and the group of airfields in the Plain of Catania, then complete the capture of the island in conjunction with the Americans. General Patton's Seventh Army was to assault between Capo Scaramia and Licata with the object of capturing the port of Licata and the group of airfields which included Ponte Olivo, Biscari, and Comiso. Seventh Army was to ensure the defence of the airfields and subsequently was to protect the left flank of Eighth Army from any enemy threats developed from the west of the island.

Intelligence regarding the layout of the Axis defences in Sicily was gradually collected and it eventually became apparent that the garrison consisted of two German armoured divisions—the 'Hermann Goering' and the

'Sicily'—and five Italian field divisions. (Shortly before our invasion the 'Sicily' Division was renamed 15 Panzer Grenadier Division.) In addition to these formations, a series of Italian coastal divisions, six in number, was disposed round the coast. The layout of the enemy's dispositions in general indicated that he considered the south-east and east to be the most likely area of assault, but that he did not dismiss the possibility of landings in the west. It was evident that he wished to safeguard against any threat to Licata and the airfield group to the north-east of it and also to Catania and its associated aerodromes. The long coastline abounded in suitable assault beaches and it was to be presumed that the coastal defence screen was designed to delay hostile landings, reliance being placed on strong counter attacks to push any invader back into the sea. On Eighth Army's sector 206 Coastal Division was strung out over nearly sixty miles of coast from Capo Campolato to Licata and was known to be poorly equipped and low in morale. I did not therefore anticipate any great difficulty in the initial assault, but appreciated that counter attacks might develop soon after and that increasingly severe opposition would be encountered in the advance towards Catania. Both the Hermann Goering and 15 Panzer Grenadier Divisions were facing the south-east corner of the island, but were split into battle groups which were very dispersed and, in view of the poor roads, it was likely to be many hours before they could concentrate. The Italian formation were also very scattered.

The estimated rate of enemy reinforcements to the island was potentially $1\frac{1}{2}$ to 2 divisions a week, but I considered this unlikely owing to maintenance limitations: which I felt would severely limit his build-up.

The defences of the assault beaches, though continuous, did not appear strong. There were short belts of barbed wire, machine gun posts, and a few pillboxes, while the artillery strength in the coastal sectors appeared to be negligible. The fighting value of the Italian troops was open to question, as none of them had been in action elsewhere and there was no reason to believe that they were above the average. But as I have already mentioned, the Italian troops fought desperately in the closing stages of the Tunisian campaign and it was reasonable to assume that they would show even more spirit in the defence of their homeland.

As is well known, the general topography of Sicily is very mountainous and movement off the roads and tracks is seldom possible. In the beach areas there was a narrow coastal plain, but behind this the mountains rose steeply and the road network was very indifferent. It was apparent that the campaign in Sicily was going to depend largely on the domination of main road and track centres and the story of the operations will show that these invariably became our main objectives.

THE EIGHTH ARMY PLAN

13 Corps was to assault immediately south of Siracusa. Its operation was planned to begin with the drop of 1 Air Landing Brigade Group west of Siracusa between 2210 and 2230 hours on 9 July in order to capture a very important bridge over the Anapo River called Ponte Grande, together with the coastal batteries north of the river and the seaplane base nearby. Commando troops were to land from the sea four hours later and capture a main coastal battery at Capo Murro di Porco. The main assault of 13 Corps would then be made by 5 Division on a two brigade front and 50 Division on a one brigade front. The former was to capture Cassibile and subsequently advance on Siracusa in co-operation with the airborne troops. 50 Division was to capture Avola and protect the Corps bridgehead from the west and south-west. The protection of the bridgehead involved securing a firm footing on the plateau some two and a half miles inland which completely dominates the coastal road between Noto and Cassibile. In the second phase 5 and 50 Divisions were to secure bridgeheads over the Simeto River and capture Catania, being relieved for this task by 30 Corps, which was to take over the initial 13

120

Corps beachhead.

30 Corps plan provided for a landing by 231 Infantry Brigade Group south of Marzamemi with the task of developing a beachhead to protect the Corps right flank; patrols were to be pushed out as rapidly as possible to gain contact with 13 Corps near Avola. 51 Division was to land in the centre on a frontage of four battalions astride the south-eastern point of the Pachino peninsula, with the immediate object of capturing the town of Pachino. On the left of 51 Division, 1 Canadian Division was to establish a beachhead protecting the Corps left flank and was made responsible for capturing the Pachino landing ground. The seizure of this airfield and its immediate rehabilitation was considered a primary Corps task and, although allotted to 1 Canadian Division, orders provided for its capture by whichever formation in the Corps made the most rapid progress.

30 Corps first main objective was the road Noto–Rosolini Spaccaforna. After its capture, 51 Division was to be prepared to relieve 50 Division (13 Corps) at Avola. The second main Corps objective was the high ground covering the convergence of road routes in the area Palazzolo–Ragusa. At the latter place 1 Canadian Division was to make contact with 2 United States Corps. The main thrust line of 30 Corps was then to be along the road axis Palazzolo–Vizzini.

Naval supporting ships were to assist the initial landings and our subsequent advances on the coastal sector. A comprehensive plan of air support was also drawn up.

FINAL PREPARATIONS FOR THE ASSAULT

On 3 July I arrived in Malta to find the whole of the Eighth Army staff installed there for the start of the invasion.

My first aim was to see Air Vice-Marshal Park in order to get from him the complete air picture. Only at this late stage were we able to make close contact with the Air Force authority responsible on our front for the assault phase. The enemy long-range bombers had been pushed well back, but there was still a formidable hostile fighter strength in Sicily and in spite of all our efforts the enemy fighters were refusing combat. But the Allied air forces were dealing with the enemy in no uncertain way and it was not likely that his air forces would cause us any great trouble.

According to my normal custom I issued a personal message to the troops, which was read out to them when they embarked. The stage was set for the operation which was to carry Eighth Army across the sea and ultimately into the mainland of Europe. The soldiers were very enthusiastic and soberly confident of the issue and so was I, although I suffered from no delusions about the serious fighting which lay ahead.

CHAPTER ELEVEN

THE ASSAULT ON SICILY, THE EXTENSION OF THE BRIDGEHEAD, AND THE ADVANCE TO THE PLAIN OF CATANIA, 10–21 JULY 1943

THE ASSAULT

During 9 July the convoys of the Seventh United States and Eighth Armies closed towards their rendezvous areas east and west of Malta. During the day the wind rose sharply in the central Mediterranean and the naval assault formations were formed up in a heavy sea, prior to the approach to the Sicilian coast where landings were due to commence in the early hours of 10 July. The swell threatened to make the beaching of assault craft and the landing of troops a hazardous undertaking and many of the men were suffering from sea sickness. During the night the invasion convoys reached the transport areas from which assault craft were to be launched, but at this time the wind began to slacken so that there was a fair hope that the gale would subside before the troops landed.

It was an anxious time, but the risk of attempting to postpone the assault until the weather became more favourable was greater than the hazard of continuing with the plan. In the event the convoys were up to schedule and reached their correct stations punctually. I would like here to pay tribute to the work of the Royal Navy in this operation. It was beyond all praise. The entire naval arrangements for landing the expedition in Sicily were brilliant.

Meanwhile in the early evening of 9 July formations of airborne forces took off from Tunisia. Unfortunately their operation did not go as planned; there was a high wind, a number of gliders fell into the sea and a large proportion of the troops landed wide of the objective. Only a very small force, therefore, reached the Ponte Grande, which was nevertheless held with remarkable heroism for nearly eighteen hours.

The seaborne assault was an outstanding success. It was greatly facilitated by the failure of the enemy air force seriously to oppose it and because, as a result of the gale, the enemy garrison, already wearied by false alerts and scares, had relaxed its vigilance. The first waves of our assault achieved complete tactical surprise and the enemy's confusion and disorganization were such that he was unable to offer any co-ordinated opposition. Some of the beaches came under sporadic fire from coastal batteries and artillery inland, but little damage was done and the guns were soon silenced; the naval supporting gunfire was admirable. By first light successful landings had been made on all our beaches.

Resistance in 30 Corps sector was very light and by 0730 hours 10 July, the rehabilitation of the Pachino airfield, which had been ploughed up, was in progress; soon after midday the strip was ready for use. By early afternoon the town of Pachino was reported clear and by the end of the day the whole of the peninsula was in our hands and a thousand prisoners had been taken. Progress was slower at first in 13 Corps sector owing to the heavy seas and a certain amount of enemy shelling, but by 1000 hours we had captured Cassibile and Casanuova and gained a footing in Avola and Noto. By the early evening 5 Division was firmly established on the plateau overlooking Cassibile and on its left 50 Division held the southern end of the same plateau north-west of Noto. On the right of 13 Corps, 5 Division reached Ponte Grande in the afternoon and succeeded in rescuing the survivors of the airborne party who had removed the charges from the bridge. As a result our troops were able to march on Siracusa without delay and captured the town undamaged.

The first day of this great amphibious enterprise had been eminently successful. All our initial objectives had been secured without enemy counter attacks or indeed serious opposition. None of the German battle groups had been able to intervene against Eighth Army and even the Italian division located near Siracusa had failed to oppose us. We had got ashore with very few casualties and the landing of troops and stores over the beaches had continued throughout the day with marked success in spite of a heavy surf. We had secured a firm foothold in the Island.

THE ADVANCE TO THE PLAIN OF CATANIA AND ENNA

On 11 July the main thrusts were initiated by 13 Corps towards Augusta and by 30 Corps on the axis Palazzolo–Vizzini. Throughout the day the discharge of ships and craft at Siracusa and on the beaches continued satisfactorily and there was every reason to believe that our build-up of reserves, vehicles, and weapons would proceed satisfactorily.

The first major enemy counter attack fell on the American sector and was delivered towards Gela by a force of about sixty German tanks. After making some progress they received a tremendous hammering and the enemy eventually lost forty-three tanks. Meanwhile contact was made between the Canadians and the right American corps in the Ragusa area.

I took my Tactical Headquarters over from Malta during the morning of 11 July and spent the day visiting the front. I was confirmed in my view that the battle of Sicily would be primarily a matter of securing the main centres of road communication. Movement off the roads and tracks in the hilly country was very difficult and often impossible, so that if the nodal points were gained it was clear that the enemy would be unable to operate.

By the end of 12 July we were firmly in possession of the south-east of the Island. 13 Corps had some trouble in securing Augusta owing to German tank counter attacks which were eventually beaten off with naval and air co-operation. The port was entered during the night 12/13 July.

Two intrepid destroyers of the Royal Navy had sailed into the harbour before the troops arrived in the town! Meanwhile 30 Corps was established on the general line Sortini–Palazzolo–Ragusa–Scicli. The operations were very exhausting for the troops, for we had not yet got any troop-carrying transport ashore, and long marches in the hot sun were most tiring. But I ordered all efforts to be made to maintain the pressure, as it was essential to take every advantage of the disorganized state of the enemy before he sorted himself out. Once left by the Germans, the Italian troops showed little fight and either surrendered after token resistance, demobilized themselves, or fled to the north. The German forces had not yet become properly concentrated or co-ordinated and, although their rearguards began to stiffen on 12 July, we were not seriously held up.

My orders on 12 July were for the advance to continue on the two axes, 13 Corps along the coast towards Catania and the north, 30 Corps to Caltagirone, Enna, and Leonforte. The Americans were advancing well, and it seemed to me that if they got established at Caltanissetta, Canicatti, and Agrigento we should be in a position to develop operations to cut off all the enemy in western Sicily.

Progress was slower on 13 July. It was very hot and the troops were getting tired, but 30 Corps made progress towards Vizzini. There was a danger of overlapping between the two armies in the area Vizzini–Caltagirone, but this was put right by orders from 15 Army Group which made the road axis through those places to Piazza Amerina and Enna inclusive to Eighth Army. On the 13 Corps flank I decided that we should make a great effort to break through into the Plain of Catania from the Lentini area and ordered a major attack for the night 13/14 July. A parachute brigade and a commando were made available for the operation, in which the main problems were to force the bottleneck through the difficult country between Carlentini and Lentini and to secure two bridges: one north of the Lentini ridge and the other, the Primasole, over the River Simeto.

The plan was to land the parachute brigade during the night near Primasole bridge with orders to capture it and establish a small bridgehead on the north bank. Contact was then to be made with the commando whose task, having landed west of Agnone, was to secure the other bridge. The main thrust, directed on Catania, was to be delivered by 50 Division with an armoured brigade leading. Naval support for the air and sea landings was arranged.

The first stages of the attack were successful and both bridges fell into our hands intact. The airborne operation was accomplished by a small part of the brigade, since only half the parachutists' aircraft dropped troops over the target and only a proportion of the gliders landed in the correct area. But the charges were removed from the bridge and the paratroops hung on until darkness on 14 July, by which time they had withstood a series of counter attacks by tanks and infantry and were becoming hard pressed. The commando meanwhile removed the charges from its bridge, but was subsequently forced to withdraw. The main body was held up in most difficult country by very strong enemy forces covering Carlentini and not until the afternoon of 14 July, when some of our tanks succeeded in working round the enemy's east flank, was our infantry able to continue the advance through Lentini. In the early hours of 15 July contact was made with the parachute brigade which had withdrawn to a ridge overlooking the plain and the Primasole bridge: which was still intact.

The enemy's rearguard action had given him time to organize firm resistance north of the Simeto and the fate of the vital bridge hung in the balance for several days. In attacks on 15 July we got some infantry and tanks temporarily across the bridge, but heavy counter attacks prevented tanks from remaining north of the river, and attempts to cross upstream were unsuccessful. By evening the bridge was still in dispute.

On 16 July before dawn a shallow bridgehead was at last established over the Simeto and by the end of the following

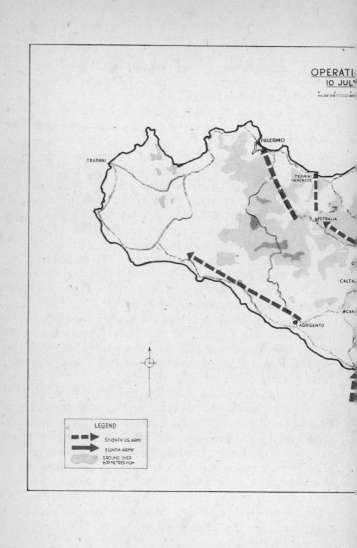

OPERATI
10 JUL

TRAPANI

PALERMO

TERMINI
IMMERESE

PETRALIA

CALTA

CAN

AGRIGENTO

LEGEND

SEVENTH US ARMY

EIGHTH ARMY

GROUND OVER
600 METRES HIGH

MAP 14

SICILY
T 1943

MESSINA
BROLO
ORLANDO
TORRE NOVA
S. STEFANO
ALI
C'O LANDING
MISTRETTA
FRANCAVILL
RANDAZZO
LINGUAGLOSS
CESARO
MALETTO
TAORMINA
TROINA
BRONTE
FIUMEFREDDO
NICOSIA
MT ETNA
LEONFORTE
ADRANO
BIANCAVILLA
CENTURIPE
ACEREALE
DITTAINO
CATENANUOVA
BELPASSO
PATERNO
ENNA
VALGUARNER
SFERRO
MISTERBIANC
CATANIA
RADDUSA
GERBINI
GULF OF
CATANIA
PIAZZA ARMERINA
PRIMA SOLE
CATANIA
LANDING
SCORDIA
AGNONE
MILITELLO
LENTINI
C CAMPOLATO
CALTAGIRONE
LENTINI
FRANCOFONTE
AUGUSTA
VIZZINI
SORTINI
PONTE OLIVO
PALAZZOLO
ANAPO
SIRACUSA
GELA
PONTE GRANDE
AIRBORNE
LANDING
BISCARI
C MURRO DI PORCO
CASSIBILE
COMISO
CASANUOLA
RAGUSA
AVOLA
NOTO
SCICLI
ROSOLINI
GULF OF
NOTO
SPACCAFORNA
CAPO SCARAMIA
POZZALLO
MARZAMEMI
PACHINO

day we were firmly over the river, with anti-tank guns and tanks in support of the infantry, holding a bridgehead some 3,000 yards deep. In spite of all the enemy's efforts to regain it, the bridge remained intact. We had now sufficient depth north of the river to mount a full scale attack towards Catania and on the night 17/18 July 50 Division launched a strong thrust northwards. Hostile resistance was firm and determined and fierce counter attacks were put in by the enemy so that little was achieved.

On my western flank 30 Corps continued to progress against stiffening opposition provided by elements of the Panzer divisions together with some paratroops. The enemy was endeavouring to hold routes open for the German troops in the west, and as the country inland became more mountainous and rugged, so the task of the attackers became more difficult. 51 Division leading the 30 Corps advance was held up at Vizzini on 13 July and the town was not in our hands until the afternoon of the next day.

Meanwhile my two main thrusts were diverging and I decided that I needed a strong pivot between them in order to preserve balance. Since 51 Division was now very tired, I ordered 30 Corps to bring 1 Canadian Division into the lead, leaving 51 Division in reserve with the task of clearing up the area Scordia–Francofonte Militello.

After the fall of Vizzini, the Canadians advanced rapidly through Caltagirone to Piazza Armerina, which fell during the night 16/17 July. Operations were then developed towards Valguarnera and Leonforte with the object of cutting the Enna–Catania road at Leonforte and tackling Enna (which was known to be in a state of defence) from the east.

On 16 July, I ordered 30 Corps to advance 51 Division towards Paterno in order to assist the operations of 13 Corps. By the end of 17 July the Division had crossed the Simeto river and was within 10 miles of Paterno, facing strong enemy positions.

The opposition was beginning to crystallize. The bulk of

Hermann Goering Division was now in the Catania Plain, and reinforcements from 1 Parachute Division had been flown in from Italy on successive nights until a total of about six battalions were in the line. Two German fortress battalions were also identified having been rushed over from the mainland.

COMMENCEMENT OF THE LEFT HOOK TOWARDS MOUNT ETNA

It had been decided on 15 July by 15 Army Group that the Seventh United States Army should develop operations northwards from Caltanissetta to Caterina and Petralia. Meanwhile with the outer flank of Eighth Army thus secured, I could thrust to Leonforte and thence eastwards on Adrano and get round the northern side of Etna. From Petralia the Americans could operate to cut the north coastal road and thus complete the isolation of the west of the Island; my thrust should get behind the enemy in the Catania area and drive a wedge between the Hermann Goering Division in the Catania Plain and 15 Panzer Grenadier Division which was getting into position on its western flank.

During 17 and 18 July the enemy's plan of action became clear. He was withdrawing the German forces into the north-east of the Island, pivoting on Catania, and was determined to hold the city and to deny us the airfields south of it. Indeed the airfields in the Plain of Catania were the greatest prize in the Island, for as soon as our Air Forces could become established on them we would not only derive greater strength for the battle, but would be able to develop air operations further afield with greater intensity. In defending Catania the enemy was greatly assisted by the ground, which was admirably suited to defence; his positions in the plain were backed by the foothills of Mount Etna which gave him excellent observation. Meanwhile on the western flank he was now developing a heavy scale of demolitions, which were skilfully related to the mountainous country and were

131

beginning to slow down the speed of operations.

Following 50 Division's attack on the night 17/18 July, 5 Division was brought round on to its left flank and on the afternoon of 18 July began thrusting towards Misterbianco, in an effort to broaden the front of our attacks on Catania and get round the core of enemy resistance there. I was now therefore operating four divisional thrusts. 13 Corps had 50 Division on the coast directed on Catania and 5 Division on its left making for Misterbianco. In 30 Corps, 51 Division was thrusting towards Paterno while 1 Canadian Division was directed on Leonforte and Adrano.

The four thrusts continued on 19 July. Progress continued to be slow, but our artillery fire and steady pressure were taking effect and the enemy's casualties were extremely heavy. 5 Division crossed the Simeto and drew level with the 50 Division bridgehead, but was unable to get further until a proper crossing place had been constructed to facilitate moving supporting weapons to the north bank. 51 Division established a bridgehead over the Dittaino River at Sferro and on 20 July captured most of the Gerbini airfield, but on the following day was thrown back by a strong enemy counter attack to positions south of the aerodrome. 1 Canadian Division, after some delay north of Valguarnera on 19 July, advanced to within a few miles of Leonforte on the following day. 231 Infantry Brigade was brought up to fill the gap between 1 Canadian and 51 Divisions and having captured Raddusa reached the Dittaino River bridge (on the road from Raddusa to Agira). On 19 July the brigade approached to within three miles of Agira itself but, as it was known to be strongly held by the enemy, 30 Corps decided not to press attacks there until Leonforte had been taken and the Agira position could be threatened from the west by the Canadians. Fierce fighting for Leonforte continued during 21 July but the town was finally surrounded and entered that night.

Meanwhile Seventh United States Army was thrusting northwards and on 22 July cut the north coast road near

Termini, while, by the same time, a series of thrusts directed north-west and west led to the capture of Palermo and the clearance of the whole of western Sicily. Many thousands of Italian prisoners were taken.

CHAPTER TWELVE

THE COMPLETION OF THE CAPTURE OF SICILY

PREPARATIONS FOR BREAKING THE GERMAN DEFENCE OF NORTH-EAST SICILY

Now that the conquest of Western Sicily had been completed, the Allied resources were concentrated on forcing the enemy out of the north-east corner of the island. It was clear that he intended to impose the maximum delay on our efforts to evict him and evidence of the arrival of further reinforcements began to be received on 20 July, when elements of 29 Panzer Grenadier Division were identified by 30 Corps. Apart from political considerations, it appeared that the Germans had three main military reasons for striving to retain their bridgehead in Sicily. The immediate purpose was to deny us, for as long as possible, use of the airfields in the Catania Plain from which we could strike with increasing weight at the heart of Italy. Secondly, it was necessary to delay us in Sicily while the German defence of Italy was organized, since it was increasingly obvious that no reliance could be placed on the Italians even in the defence of their own country. Finally, the escape route to the mainland had to be held open for the time when fighting in Sicily could not be prolonged. We had therefore to face fierce and protracted resistance.

The topography of north-east Sicily greatly favoured the enemy. It was possible for him to organize a series of very strong delaying positions all the way to Messina and there was no opportunity of exploiting in mass our superiority in armoured forces. In the weeks ahead we were daily planning to land forces from the sea behind the enemy and indeed, success was achieved in this way, but beaches were scarce and generally unsuitable for the deployment of any but minor forces. Moreover, the availability of landing craft was greatly restricted, since they were being overhauled in preparation for the invasion of the Italian mainland. In the air, our mounting offensive was achieving outstanding success and not only were we virtually unhindered by enemy aircraft, but we were able to keep up a relentless pounding of the hostile troops and of communication.

The enemy ultimately employed four German divisions in the Island: 29 Panzer Grenadier Division on the northern sector of his defences, 15 Panzer Grenadier Division in the centre, and Hermann Goering Division in the east. 1 Parachute Division did not operate independently, but provided detachments at various key points. Remnants of three Italian divisions remained fighting with the Germans.

Our own troops had been constantly engaged since the landing and were beginning to show definite signs of fatigue owing to the intense July heat and continual marching over the mountainous country. On 20 July I ordered 78 Division to be brought over from Sousse, in order to increase my offensive power, since all my available divisions in Sicily were now deployed in the line.

On 21 July I decided that it was necessary to shift the main weight of the Eighth Army offensive to the left flank. It was by then quite clear that the enemy was going to hold Catania to the last and to persist with the direct advance on that axis would result in heavy casualties which I could not afford. A better approach would be to pass round the north of Mount Etna and come in behind him. I would give 78 Division to 30 Corps in order to capture first Centuripe and then Adrano and afterwards swing north to Bronte and Randazzo. Meanwhile it was essential to provide more aerodromes for the Royal Air Force, in order to increase the weight of air attack on the enemy: our object being to isolate Sicily from the mainland, smash the key road centres to the island and demoralize the hostile troops.

I therefore ordered that 13 Corps front and 51 Division

of 30 Corps should revert to the defensive, maintaining aggressive patrol activity and raids in order to pin the opposing enemy formations in their existing positions. The left flank of 30 Corps was to be my main thrust and the target date for the full scale drive on the enemy was fixed as 1 August, by which time I hoped to have 78 Division ready for action. In the meantime, I directed 30 Corps to continue operations on the axes Leonforte–Agira–Regalbuto and Catenanuova–Centuripe in order to get within striking distance of Adrano which I reasoned was the key to the Mount Etna position.

On my left, Seventh United States Army was regrouping for the drive on Messina and Army Group orders provided for the development of two divisional thrusts (the maximum strength which could be maintained in the sector) along the roads Nicosia–Troina–Randazzo and Termini Immerese–San Stefano–Cape d'Orlando. 1 August was set as the target date for these drives to develop from the line Nicosia–Mistretta–San Stefano.

THE ADVANCE EAST FROM LEONFORTE

After the fall of Leonforte the enemy continued to resist 30 Corps advance fiercely. 1 Canadian Division was held up east of the town and again in front of Nissoria, which was cleared on 24 July. Meanwhile 231 Infantry Brigade was attacking towards Agira from the south but, having succeeded in cutting the main road east of the town, was forced to withdraw in face of strong counter-attacks. Very heavy fighting continued round Agira until 28 July, when it fell into our hands.

Meanwhile 78 Division was brought into the line in the Catenanuova area and together with a Canadian brigade launched an attack on the town on the night 29/30 July. After fierce fighting Catenanuova was cleared early in the morning and a further attack the following night cleared the high ground to the north and north-east, thus providing us with an adequate bridgehead from which to launch an operation against Centuripe. This place, built on a very high mountain mass and reached by a single road which twists and turns up the steep side of the feature, presented an extremely difficult objective. However, during the night 1/2 August leading troops of 78 Division entered the town, but they were forced to withdraw at first light when the enemy was found to be in the houses in considerable strength. An attack to dislodge the Germans was mounted the following day and eventually on the morning of 3 August, we took full possession of the town, the enemy having fallen back across the Salso river.

The storming of Centuripe was a fine achievement and reflected the greatest credit on 78 Division, for its capture was the essential preliminary to the battle of Adrano. With Centuripe in our possession the fall of Adrano was a certainty. We now dominated the approaches to a key point in the enemy's Etna position. Its fall would mean that the end of the campaign in Sicily could not be long delayed.

Following the fall of Agira 231 Infantry Brigade led the west flank advance towards Regalbuto. Road blocks impeded progress but no serious resistance was met until the morning of 30 July on the outskirts of Regalbuto itself. Operations on the night 30/31 July were only partially successful owing to strong enemy counter attacks and, after severe fighting throughout 31 July, our troops were still a mile west of the objective. The Canadian Division was brought up from Agira and after more hard fighting during 1 August the town was entered late in the afternoon and occupied in force the following morning, by which time the leading troops were three miles to the east.

During the development of operations on the western flank, 13 Corps continued its activities in order to pin down enemy forces on its front. In the centre sector I had ordered 13 Corps on 22 July, to take over the front of the right hand brigade of 30 Corps in order to provide additional resources for the main thrust. The front of 5 Division was increased accordingly. I anticipated that the enemy might attack towards Sferro as a natural reaction to my advance on the Adrano axis and on 29 July ordered reinforcements of two infantry battalions (provided from Beach Bricks) and a regiment of Canadian tanks to be sent to the left of 5 Division. 51 Division continued to maintain balance between the two Corps.

At the end of the month we made a most interesting capture of a map of enemy dispositions which clearly showed that Adrano was indeed the key to the German Etna position, confirming that it was correct to launch the main Eighth Army thrust towards that place, for once we could smash the Adrano hinge the Etna position would disintegrate.

At this stage I was considering the regrouping necessary for carrying the war on to the mainland of Italy. There were two separate Corps operations under consideration for the invasion of the 'toe' by Eighth Army. 10 Corps was waiting in the Tripoli area. I had already discussed with the Commander, General Horrocks, its possible role in Calabria. I now turned to the grouping of 13 Corps and decided that it would be used for the direct crossing of the Straits of Messina. For this purpose 1 Canadian and 5 Divisions would be required in the assault, while 78 Division would be held available as the immediate reserve. Once the war in Sicily was over it would be necessary to rest 50 and 51 Divisions which had been fighting hard since El Alamein, and it was therefore my intention to finish the 'Husky' operation with 30 Corps (consisting of 50, 51, and 78 Divisions) as soon as the two thrusts around Mount Etna met in the north. This would enable me to rest and refit 1 Canadian and 5 Divisions during the last phase in Sicily.

THE FALL OF CATANIA AND RANDAZZO

On 4 August I gave orders to the Corps concerning the future conduct of operations. 30 Corps was to continue the drive on Adrano. In 13 Corps, 50 Division was to be ready to seize Catania when the opportunity came and 5 Division, after taking Misterbianco, was to be directed on Belpasso. I stipulated that 13 Corps would maintain an infantry brigade with a tank regiment on the Sferro—Paterno axis where it was essential to provide a firm link. After the fall of Adrano 30 Corps was to revert 1 Canadian Division to reserve and, following the capture of Belpasso, 13 Corps was to place 5 Division in reserve. These formations could then commence planning and refitting for the invasion of Italy. Subsequent operations would be conducted east of Mount Etna by 13 Corps with 50 Division and on the west by 30 Corps directed on Randazzo with 51 and 78 Divisions. When the two corps met north of the mountain, 30 Corps would take command of 50 Division and complete the 'Husky' operation, Headquarters 13 Corps coming out of the line in preparation for the attack on the mainland.

The advance of 30 Corps beyond Centuripe and Regalbuto directly threatened the main enemy Etna position and was beginning to endanger the troops holding up 13 Corps in the Catania area. It became clear on 3 August that the enemy had commenced thinning out in the Catania sector with the object of withdrawing the bulk of the German forces to the north. 5 Division attacked on the night 3/4 August on a two brigade front and by the following afternoon an advance of about four miles had been made. In the immediate coastal sector extensive demolitions and mines considerably hindered movement and on the 50 Division front a fierce rearguard action was fought in the southern outskirts of Catania, astride the main coast road. During 5 August, however, advances were made throughout the 13 Corps front and Catania, Misterbianco, and Paterno were captured. East of Mount Etna the main enemy force withdrew to new positions on a narrow front north of Acireale.

Meanwhile 30 Corps closed in on Adrano which was relentlessly pounded from the air. 78 Division crossed the Salso river astride the Centuripe—Adrano road during the night 4/5 August while 1 Canadian Division made another crossing on its left. The attack was pressed in face of strong resistance and on 6 August 78 Division reached the southern outskirts of Adrano, while patrols by-passed it and got close to the Bronte road north of the town. During the night 6/7 August the enemy withdrew and 78 Division took possession of the place and, on the following morning, turned north to follow up the enemy towards Bronte. The advance was now very slow owing to mines and demolitions and the extreme difficulty of deploying off the very indifferent road which ran through extensive lava belts and terraced cultivation.

On the right of 30 Corps 51 Division operated towards Biancavilla which was captured on 6 August.

With the fall of Adrano the main defence line across north-eastern Sicily was broken and the enemy was now in retreat on all sectors. But it was extremely difficult to follow him up closely and he continued to impede our progress with widespread and skilful demolitions. The Air Force, however, were able to inflict heavy damage and casualties on the retreating columns. Aerial reconnaissance now began to reveal increasing traffic across the Straits of Messina, from which we inferred that the enemy was beginning to send back to the mainland his rearguard installations and equipment. It became a matter of first importance for our naval and air forces to prevent this evacuation.

At dawn 8 August, 78 Division entered Bronte and to the east of Mount Etna 50 Division was fighting some eight miles north of Catania. Meanwhile United States forces had had a fierce battle round Troina ending with its capture on 6 August, and two days later entered Cesaro, whence operations were continued along the main road towards Randazzo.

At this time I was moving my Tactical Headquarters with 30 Corps, intending to switch to the 13 Corps axis when we got east of Randazzo.

North of Bronte progress continued to be very slow. South of Maletto the enemy was encountered in some strength and it was not until 12 August that the town itself

140

and the high ground in its vicinity were captured. The following day Seventh United States Army attacked Randazzo.

Returning to the eastern flank, I had decided on 9 August to modify my orders to 13 Corps concerning the advance on a single divisional front east of Mount Etna. My original idea was to get 5 Division in reserve to prepare for the invasion of Italy. Had the advance to Randazzo been quicker the threat to cut off the forces east of the mountain would have developed earlier and enabled 13 Corps to advance without undue difficulty. When it became apparent however that the Randazzo operation was going to take time, indeed that the enemy was reinforcing that sector from his coastal axis, it became essential for 13 Corps to drive hard along the coast and I ordered it to bring 5 Division forward into the line again so as to operate on a two divisional front. I wanted to get firm control of the triangle Francavilla–Taormina–Fiumefreddo and, if it was going to be difficult to get round the west side of Etna, I would force my way round the east; for it was obviously vital to cut the southern approach to Messina as quickly as possible. On 11 August I decided on further regrouping, because the target date for landing in the toe of Italy was now advanced to 1 September. I therefore ordered that 51 Division should relieve 5 Division and that Headquarters 30 Corps should take over the responsibilities of Headquarters 13 Corps on 13 August. I could no longer delay getting the invasion force for Italy into reserve.

THE FINAL PHASE IN SICILY

The Americans captured Randazzo on 13 August, at which time 78 Division was fighting strongly to the south of the town. The fall of Randazzo presaged the final elimination of the enemy from Sicily, but progress from now on was still inevitably slow as the Allied forces had to follow up along coastal roads from which deployment was almost impossible.

On 14 August the enemy had broken contact at all points

on the Eighth Army front and on the following day 50 Division occupied Taormina. 51 Division secured Linguaglossa and 78 Division cleared the lateral road from Randazzo to the coast.

During this time, on the north coast road Seventh United States Army had progressed east of Capo d'Orlando, having carried out two amphibious operations between Torrenova and Brolo in order to cut off the retreating enemy and accelerate the speed of advance.

I gave orders for a landing in front of 30 Corps on the night 15/16 August, which was successfully accomplished by a commando with some tanks at Ali, but the enemy had already withdrawn north of the area before the landing was made. Owing to demolitions on the Corniche road the force was unable to advance either to the north or south and a party moved inland on foot, seeking a route across country to Messina.

American troops entered Messina on the night of 16 August, while enemy batteries on the Calabrian peninsula intermittently shelled the town. On the following morning elements of the commando which had landed at Ali joined the Americans.

The fall of Messina marked the end of the Sicilian campaign which had cost the Germans 24,000 killed.

Eighth Army now looked out across the lovely straits of Messina towards the 'toe' of Italy, while it prepared to carry the war into the mainland of Europe. The Sicilian campaign had lasted thirty-eight days and had involved fierce and continuous fighting in most difficult country at the hottest season of the year. For a second time the Germans had been pushed back into the sea and we now stood at the gates of the 'Fortress of Europe'.

REFLECTIONS ON THE SICILIAN CAMPAIGN

Axis strategy in Sicily had been faulty to a degree. The Allies had achieved complete tactical surprise in the landing and we had caught the German forces very dispersed.

Failure of the Italian troops to show any serious opposition, combined with the action of the Air Forces in hindering the use of the indifferent road network, had imposed great delay on the concentration of the German formations and we had become very firmly established in the Island before the opposition crystallized against us. The subsequent development of the campaign had been quite straightforward from our point of view and, considering the extremely difficult nature of the country, had been brought to a close very speedily.

The hardest fought battle in the campaign was at Primasole bridge; it may have seemed curious that, having won that battle, I switched my main axis of operations from the coastal plain leading to Catania across to the inland route leading to Adrano. Yet to persist in the thrust towards Catania would have meant very heavy casualties and I was by no means convinced that success would follow this expenditure of life. Furthermore, I did not wish to blunt the weapon when it was clear that much hard fighting lay ahead on the mainland of Europe. The object could be achieved with less loss of life by operating on the Adrano axis, with the added advantage that on that flank we would be in close touch with our American Allies.

The Eighth Army had been born, trained and grown to manhood in the North African deserts and it was a source of great satisfaction to me that it adapted itself so readily to the very difficult conditions existing in Sicily. This confirmed my view that once a fighting machine has been trained thoroughly in the basic principles of warfare, it will have no great difficulty in operating successfully in whatever conditions of climate and terrain it may have to face. It is of course essential that commanders on all levels should be versatile and mentally robust and that they should not adhere rigidly to preconceived tactical methods.

CHAPTER THIRTEEN

ADMINISTRATION IN THE SICILY CAMPAIGN

Although the campaign in Sicily lasted thirty-eight days only, the administrative problems involved both in mounting the expedition and during the campaign itself were of great interest. For the staffs and troops of Eighth Army this operation marked the opening of a new phase in the war and for the first time we tackled a combined operation involving a large scale assault on a hostile and defended coast. The experience gained in Sicily was to prove most valuable in solving the administrative problems of the subsequent campaigns in Italy and Normandy.

The preparation of a large scale combined operation provides an immense task of calculation and organization for the administrative staff. I have already shown that the planning for the Sicily operation was started before the campaign in North Africa had been brought to an end. The unusual complexity of the problem may therefore be well imagined.

The invasion of Sicily was the first occasion in this war in which large forces had been maintained over open beaches for a considerable period. In the Eighth Army we planned to capture the port of Siracusa as quickly as possible after the assault and in fact it was in our hands within 48 hours. This enabled us to reduce the period of beach maintenance considerably, although we continued to land personnel and stores over the beaches astride the Pachino peninsula for some time. The Seventh United States Army, on the other hand, depended upon beach maintenance for a much longer period. During the planning stage there were many who expressed the gravest doubts as to the wisdom of depending

144

upon beach maintenance, but there was no alternative to the acceptance of the risks involved once the decision had been made to land the Eastern and Western Task Forces side by side. In the event experience in Sicily showed that large forces can be maintained for long periods over open beaches, given adequate resources in landing craft and specialized equipment and reasonably favourable conditions of tide and weather.

An essential difference between the Sicilian campaign and that which Eighth Army had fought in North Africa, was that maintenance had to be carried out over indifferent roads through enclosed country. In the desert there was no limit to the number of vehicles which could move along the desert tracks, but in Sicily the roads were narrow, steep, and tortuous and traffic control assumed greater importance than ever before. Special measures were devised to control the movement of convoys, to limit the number and class of vehicles on the roads and to deal with the problem of civilian traffic. This experience again stood us in good stead in subsequent campaigns.

The bridging problem came to the fore in Sicily as a result of the wide scale of demolitions practised by the enemy. Fortunately plans for the provision of bridging equipment had been made on a generous scale and large quantities of Bailey bridging were landed at an early date.

Another major problem in Sicily arose from the prevalence of malaria. This had been foreseen, but despite all possible precautions the casualties from malaria exceeded those incurred in battle. The disease was particularly rampant in the Plain of Catania.

Yet another aspect of the arrangements for the Sicilian campaign, which provided invaluable experience for the future, was the evolution of a special inter-Service staff machinery for controlling the loading and despatch of convoys subsequent to the assault. A plan is, of course, essential for the loading of the follow-up and build-up convoys, but this has to be made before the operation and in the event elasticity is essential to ensure that supporting troops, reserves, reinforcements, and stores are called forward in the order required by the operational situation. This inter-Service staff was originally called 'Ferry Control'. In the North West European campaign the name was changed to 'Build Up Control'.

The maintenance plan to support the operations of Eighth Army in Sicily was worked out at Allied Force Headquarters in North Africa. After the initial period scheduled supply convoys were arranged from the United Kingdom and the Middle East, while ordnance stores were provided from the depots in North Africa. There was a division of responsibility, particularly between North Africa and Headquarters Middle East Forces, but a smooth system of working was quickly established. There was no intention to set up base depots or workshops in Sicily as the campaign was too short to justify their establishment. It is not possible, however, to keep the maintenance of a modern army at concert pitch unless it is in close contact with its base, and difficulties arose which increased considerably during the initial stages of the Italian campaign.

In speaking of the maintenance arrangements made for the final phase in North Africa I mentioned the question of administrative control. This matter became very prominent in Sicily. The special administrative headquarters which I had set up in Tripoli to look after my lines of communication and to provide for my requirements had carried out these functions satisfactorily. The Headquarters itself formed part of the Eighth Army administrative machine, and I was therefore anxious to carry it with me so that it could perform the same function in Sicily. This was eventually done, the headquarters being called 'Fortbase'. Headquarters 15 Army Group had only a small administrative staff in Sicily, designed to ensure co-ordination between the two armies, to control the ferry service, and to provide the

Army Group Commander with administrative advice. While this arrangement worked satisfactorily in Sicily it became very difficult to operate in Italy and eventually had to be changed.

THE INVASION OF THE MAINLAND OF ITALY AND THE ADVANCE TO THE RIVER SANGRO 3 SEPTEMBER–31 DECEMBER 1943

CHAPTER FOURTEEN

PLANNING THE INVASION OF ITALY

THE EVOLUTION OF THE PLAN

I have already mentioned that there were originally two separate operations under consideration for the invasion of Italy by the Eighth Army. The first was known as Operation 'Buttress', which provided for a landing in the area of Gioia Taur on the north coast of the 'toe', and the other was called Operation 'Baytown' in which the plan was to make a direct crossing of the Straits of Messina.

Towards the end of July 1943 a third plan (Operation 'Avalanche') designed for a landing near Naples began to receive consideration. It was immediately apparent that our resources in craft and shipping would not permit three different assault landing operations. By 17 August, when the Sicilian campaign finished, it had been decided that 'Buttress' would not take place, but that the Italian mainland would be invaded across the Straits of Messina by Eighth Army and subsequently in the Bay of Salerno by Fifth United States Army. 10 Corps was placed under command of Fifth Army and I was therefore left with 13 and 30 Corps for Operation 'Baytown'. The target date for my operation was 30/31 August, and 'Avalanche' was to follow on 10 September. It has been seen that planning for biting off the 'toe' of Italy had been going on for some time within the Eighth Army and that, before the end of the war in Sicily, I had withdrawn formations into reserve so that they could refit and prepare themselves for the next phase of our operations.

I set in motion the preparations for invading Italy with

maximum speed, as it was essential to follow up the enemy as quickly as possible before he had time to improve his arrangements for our reception on the far side of the Straits. 30 Corps artillery began concentrating in the Messina area in order to commence the preparatory bombardment of the enemy defences and to support the assault when the time came. Intensive work was carried out on the roads and railways in Sicily in order to improve the administrative axes which we would require in the island and the formations of 13 Corps began detailed planning for carrying out the assault landing.

The object given to me for Operation 'Baytown' was as follows:—

'Your task is to secure a bridgehead on the "toe" of Italy to enable our Naval forces to operate through the Straits of Messina. In the event of the enemy withdrawing from the "toe" you will follow him up with such force as you can make available, bearing in mind that the greater the extent to which you can engage enemy forces in the southern "toe" of Italy, the more assistance you will be giving to "Avalanche".'

The preparation of the operation proved by no means a simple and straightforward matter and my chief difficulties arose over the question of availability of naval craft for the assault and subsequent build-up of my forces on the mainland. 'Avalanche' was given priority of resources since it was a larger operation than 'Baytown' and involved a much longer sea passage. The initial interpretation of this priority reduced the craft available for Eighth Army to an assault lift for some four equivalent battalions, with a very slow build-up. Available intelligence on the other hand made it necessary to prepare for a landing which would be opposed by German troops. 29 Panzer Grenadier Division was known to be defending the Straits together with Italian troops and 26 Panzer Division had been located behind it. In these circumstances it seemed to me that to reduce the assaulting forces to the strength of a major raid would be to risk disaster and I made urgent requests for additional resources.

In order to achieve the object of the operation, I considered it necessary to assault on a frontage of two divisions, with tanks, and to secure the Catanzaro 'neck' as the first main objective. This 'neck' formed the narrowest part of south-western Italy, between the Gulf of Squillace and the Gulf of S. Eufemia, and, if firmly occupied, would give us a proper footing on the Italian mainland and open the Straits for the Navy.

On 23 August a conference of the Commanders-in-Chief was held at Algiers where I explained my plan. This was accepted and the necessary additional resources were allotted to the Eighth Army.

By this time it was too late to launch Operation 'Baytown' at the end of August as had originally been planned, and eventually the target date was set for the night 2/3 September. It was at this conference that I heard some details concerning negotiations which were being carried on with the Italian Government about armistice terms. It was planned that following the Eighth Army's invasion of the mainland and immediately preceding Operation 'Avalanche', the Italian Government would broadcast concurrently with the Allies acceptance of armistice terms and would give instructions that all Italian resistance would cease. It was hoped that this action would so undermine the position of the Germans in Italy that they would be forced to withdraw from the country. But there were in Italy at this time some fifteen German divisions and it remained to be seen what their reaction would be. I considered it very unwise to assume that the Allied task in invading the Italian mainland would be an easy one or that the Italian armistice would necessarily presage the collapse of German resistance in Italy. On my own front I sent small parties across the Straits to land at various points in an attempt to find out the exact

153

situation regarding the opposition and the attitude of the Italians. On the night 27/28 August a party landed at Bova Marina and found the place deserted; a prisoner brought back said that the Italian population had fled into the hills and that Italian soldiers were deserting and joining the civilians. I followed this up with other small parties sent to various places, but nearly all of them failed to return. I therefore decided that Operation 'Baytown' would have to go forward as a properly staged assault and that we could not afford to take risks nor make hasty assumptions for which we had no tangible proof.

THE OUTLINE PLAN

I originally envisaged using 13 Corps for the assault. 30 Corps would support the landings from Sicily and subsequently take over the Reggio area, in order to release 13 Corps for the advance inland. This project I abandoned, owing to shortage of craft and the consequent slow rate of build-up which would have resulted in great administrative problems. I decided to use initially 13 Corps only and my orders provided for an assault on a two division front immediately north of Reggio, 1 Canadian Division on the right and 5 Division on the left. 30 Corps artillery positioned round Messina would support the assault together with a heavy weight of air attack. The main objective was the Catanzaro 'neck' and I decided that the main thrust would be made by 5 Division along the north coast road axis, while 1 Canadian Division would advance along the road San Stefano–Delianuova–Cittanova. Two commandos and 231 Infantry Brigade Group were to be held at Riposto in Sicily ready for mounting seaborne hooks along the north coast of the 'toe' as required. There were insufficient bridging resources to develop operations along the south coastal road axis and I therefore instructed 13 Corps to establish a block south of Reggio in order to secure the southern flank against enemy interference.

By 26 August the deployment of 30 Corps artillery had been completed. It included eighty medium guns and forty-eight American heavy guns lent by Seventh United States Army.

CHAPTER FIFTEEN

THE ASSAULT ON CALABRIA, THE ADVANCE TO THE CATANZARO 'NECK', AND DEVELOPMENT OF OPERATIONS TO POTENZA, 3–19 SEPTEMBER 1943

THE ASSAULT

At 0430 hours on 3 September, under cover of air action and artillery bombardment, the leading troops of 13 Corps landed on the beaches between Reggio and Villa San Giovanni. The Italian coastal troops and their supporting artillery surrendered after firing a few shots and the only German fire reported was spasmodic long range shelling from guns sited inland. These were quickly silenced by air attack. Early in the morning Reggio was captured, together with the airfield immediately to the south and San Giovanni was in our hands at 1130 hours. During the day there was no contact with German troops and by evening 1 Canadian Division had reached San Stefano and 5 Division was in Scilla. The beaches and roads were not mined, the inhabitants proved friendly and it was gratifying to find that the port of Reggio was not greatly damaged.

I ordered a landing on the north coast for the night 3/4 September at Bagnara which was successfully carried out by commando units; they succeeded in getting behind the German forces which were now opposing our advance along the coast road. Contact between the commandos and 5 Division was soon established in Bagnara, although owing to the heavy demolitions only troops on foot were able to enter the town.

It is necessary to realize throughout the story of our operations in Italy the important part which demolitions played in the campaign. The roads in Calabria and southern

Italy proper twist and turn in the mountainous country and are admirable feats of engineering; they abound in bridges, viaducts, culverts, and even tunnels and thus offer unlimited scope to military engineers for demolitions and road blocks of every conceivable kind. The Germans took the fullest advantage of this fact and our advance throughout was barred and delayed by demolitions on the widest possible scale: carried out both on the rail and road axes. On the railways, not content with the destruction of bridges, the enemy frequently resorted to the systematic blowing of each individual rail, together with ploughing up the sleepers and railway bed by means of a machine specially made for the purpose. These demolitions were skilfully sited with respect to the difficult country so that it was normally almost impossible to circumvent them. Our progress in Italy demands a great tribute to the sappers for their speed in constructing usable routes and to the resourcefulness of the troops who managed to forge ahead in spite of the frequency with which they met obstacles.

THE ADVANCE TO CATANZARO

On the axis of 1 Canadian Division progress was slow owing to road blocks, but by the end of 4 September the road running south to Melito had been cut. The subsequent advance proved so difficult that on 6 September I ordered 13 Corps to switch the Canadians to the south coast road and to proceed along it directed on Catanzaro. Prior to this, patrols had pushed south from Reggio to Bova Marina and it became clear that the enemy had completely evacuated the southern part of the 'toe'. The advance of 5 Division along the north coast road was held up north of Bagnara on 5 September by enemy rearguards. General Dempsey intended to put 231 Infantry Brigade Group ashore that night at Gioia but owing to a storm this operation was cancelled; however, 5 Division secured the place by noon 6 September. I ordered 13 Corps to advance 5 Division with 231 Infantry Brigade under command on Nicastro.

157

On the night 7/8 September a successful landing operation was carried out at Pizzo by 231 Infantry Brigade, which got behind the enemy rearguard and destroyed some transport. On both coast axes the advance continued to the line Catanzaro—Nicastro, which was reached by 10 September. Extensive reconnaissance was then pushed forward by both divisions with the particular object of reporting the situation at the port of Crotone and the airfields situated nearby. At the Catanzaro 'neck' it was necessary for me to have a short pause, for we had advanced 100 miles in seven days and were getting very strung out. Maintenance difficulties were beginning to appear owing to the delays imposed upon transport echelons on the heavily damaged roads. Moreover, the rate of our build-up was not providing us with the number of L of C units and transport columns we required in order to continue at this pace.

THE ITALIAN ARMISTICE AND THE LANDING AT SALERNO

At 1800 hours 8 September the armistice with Italy was announced. In the previous two years the main objects of Allied strategy in the Mediterranean had been to clear North Africa of Axis forces and to knock Italy out of the war. Both had now been accomplished.

At the same time we were involved in operations in Italy on two separate fronts. In the early hours of 9 September, Fifth U.S. Army landed in the Gulf of Salerno and began operations which had as their immediate object the capture of Naples; on the Eighth Army front by 10 September we had secured the line of the Catanzaro 'neck' and were preparing for further advances to assist the Salerno landing by pinning down the German forces in Calabria.

My next objects were to secure the port of Crotone in order to ease the maintenance situation, and to establish the Desert Air Force on the Crotone group of airfields. I therefore ordered 13 Corps to move 5 Division forward to the line Spezzano—Belvedere on 14 September, followed in about two days by the Canadian Division which was to be directed to the area Carati–Savelli–San Giovanni. These moves would establish my leading troops in the Castrovillari 'neck' and cover our interests in the Crotone area.

After midnight on 10 September I received a message from General Alexander concerning Operation 'Avalanche'. He emphasized the importance of maintaining the pressure against the Germans on my front to prevent their reinforcing the opposition to Fifth Army. At the same time he told me of the intention to land troops at Taranto, where by 15 September we were due to have eight thousand men put ashore from naval ships. Eighth Army was administratively very stretched at this time but I had to take every justifiable risk in order that my front could give assistance to Fifth Army operations.

THE PLAN OF ADVANCE TO POTENZA

My object was now to get forward as quickly as possible in order to pin down the enemy and to initiate without delay a threat to the southern flank of the Germans opposing the Salerno bridgehead.

The problem was to achieve these results at a time when administratively it was quite impossible for me to move major forces forward until additional resources, including transport companies and rearguard units and installations, had been provided. The shortage of craft and shipping available to the Eighth Army made the build-up relatively very slow; we were being kept at a minimum owing to other demands of higher priority.

I decided that there were three measures immediately possible. First, I ordered light forces to be despatched north of the Catanzaro 'neck' at once, with instructions to operate as far ahead as possible. Secondly, I accelerated the provision of resources for the establishment of the Desert Air Force in the Crotone area, whence air action could be developed against the Germans opposing the Salerno bridgehead and against any enemy column which might be switched from my front to the north. The action of the air, together with my light forces, would quickly make apparent to the enemy that we were pressing forward and cause him to fear for the safety of his southern flank. This threat would be accentuated by the landings at Taranto, where leading elements of 1 Airborne Division arrived on 9 September. Thirdly, I required to open Crotone port as quickly as possible to ease the administrative situation by eliminating the long and slow carry by road from Reggio.

Events developed quickly on 11 September. Crotone port was secured and found to be undamaged, meanwhile light forces reached the general line Castrovillari–Belvedere before dark. By taking considerable administrative risks I planned to concentrate all 5 Division in to the Castrovillari 'neck' by 15 September and to order the Canadian Division forward to the area Rossano–Spezzano by 17 September. At the same time I drove the forward elements further north to the limit of their supplies.

THE TARANTO BRIDGEHEAD

On 13 September I was asked by 15 Army Group to take command of the Taranto bridgehead as soon as it could be arranged.

The landing at Taranto was one of a number of plans which had been considered in connection with the anticipated change of front of the Italian forces, for the original conception of the Italian armistice was that they would turn against the Germans and assist in evicting them from the country. When this suggestion was put to me early in September I expressed doubts about the ability of the Italians seriously to influence events in the way it was hoped, and gave as my opinion that it would be unwise to count initially on effective fighting support from the proposed co-belligerents. It seemed to me dangerous, particularly in view of our shortage of shipping and resources, to make a series of weak landings in Italy on the assumption that the Italian forces would rally and fight with them. Such a course might involve us in very dangerous commitments which we would

160

be unable to support.

Ultimately only the Taranto operation was carried out. 1 Airborne Division on 9 September began unopposed landings from naval ships, with the object of securing the port, airfields, and installations in the area. Our troops were without supporting artillery and had very little transport, but the German garrison in south-east Italy, 1 Parachute Division, strung out between Foggia and Taranto, was only 8,000 strong.

A weak perimeter was established round Taranto and beyond it patrols were sent to a depth of about 40 miles to locate the German forces and contact the Italian garrisons. There were minor clashes with the enemy, but no serious opposition was encountered, as the Germans withdrew to the north and formed a perimeter line covering Altamura–Matera–Ginosa.

It was planned to follow up the Airborne Division by Headquarters 5 Corps and 8 Indian Division, which were to be sent from Egypt.

I agreed to accept responsibility for the Taranto bridgehead at once. This step enabled me to authorize certain adjustments of craft allocation to be made between the sea routes to Crotone and Taranto in order to accelerate the arrival of certain essential stores at Crotone and thus to assist the speed of 13 Corps advance towards the Salerno battle area. At the same time, after consultation with General Allfrey (commanding 5 Corps) I ordered the despatch of elements of 78 Division from Sicily to the Taranto front, including the divisional reconnaissance regiment and a field artillery regiment. These units were later followed by the rest of the Division.

THE CAPTURE OF POTENZA AND AULETTA

During the period 13–15 September, the situation at Salerno remained serious and we continued our efforts to solve our maintenance difficulties in order to speed up the advance. 5 Division was to commence concentrating in the

Belvedere area on 14 September, but I ordered 13 Corps to push a brigade ahead to Sapri, from which light forces could operate to the north. From Sapri I would be able directly to threaten the German forces opposing the southern flank of Fifth Army bridgehead.

The enemy resistance to our advance was not strong during this phase and the main difficulty operationally continued to be the extensive demolitions, which demanded ever-increasing resources in engineers and engineering material.

On 15 September additional craft for ferry work and extra transport companies were put at my disposal by Army Group and I was able to plan a further speed up of operations. I instructed 13 Corps to send detachments of 5 Division north along the road Sapri–Agropoli to endeavour to contact the right flank of Fifth United States Army. At the same time I sent to General Clark to tell him of this move. By 16 September I planned to have my leading troops on the western flank up to the line Sapri–Lagonegro while bringing 1 Canadian Division into the Castrovillari area. With the extra maintenance resources now available I decided to order the advance of main bodies to the general line Potenza–Auletta to commence on 17 September. This still involved considerable administrative risks, but they had to be accepted.

Leading elements of Eighth Army were now operating at great distances in advance of the main bodies and the threat to the Germans opposing Fifth United States Army had developed well. On 16 September contact was made between troops of 5 Division and American patrols near Vallo and at the same time Canadian reconnaissance elements met patrols sent out from the Taranto bridgehead. The enemy rearguards of 26 Panzer Division withdrew north through Lagonegro. The enemy was swinging back the southern sector of his line facing the Salerno front and on 17 September the withdrawal of enemy forces continued to the north. The immediate crisis at Salerno had passed and the bridgehead there was now to be steadily strengthened and developed.

By 19 September leading troops of 5 Division reached Auletta while the Canadians secured Potenza after driving out the German garrison belonging to 1 Parachute Division.

Eighth Army had advanced nearly 300 miles in seventeen days. The country favoured the German rearguards who were by now well practised in demolitions. The task of our sappers was enormous. Moreover, considerable administrative risks had been taken, but we had been ordered to make all haste and I think we made faster time than the enemy had bargained for. We may perhaps never know fully what effect the news of our approach had upon the enemy forces pinning down the Allied bridgehead at Salerno. On their admission, however, the Germans felt unable to continue that enterprise in face of the growing threat from the south and began to disengage.

Meanwhile in the Taranto sector, Tactical Headquarters 5 Corps had already landed, and leading units of 78 Division were due shortly to arrive at Bari.

CHAPTER SIXTEEN

THE DEVELOPMENT OF ALLIED STRATEGY IN ITALY AND THE ADVANCE OF EIGHTH ARMY TO THE RIVER SANGRO

THE GENERAL SITUATION IN ITALY ON 20 September 1943

The pattern of Allied strategy in Italy was now beginning to emerge. A bridgehead had been secured at Salerno and from Taranto we were forming a firm base which was rapidly growing in strength. Between these two pivots and in contact with them, 13 Corps was becoming established in the Potenza–Auletta area.

The Italian armistice had not seriously prejudiced the German position in Italy. Very firm measures were taken by the enemy to prevent the Italian Army endangering his hold on the country and a new Fascist regime was instituted in the German zone to supplant the Badoglio Government and to ensure retention of dictatorial powers over the population and available resources. The enemy's intentions in Italy were not entirely clear at this stage, except that he was determined to deny us the port of Naples as long as possible. In the central and eastern sectors of the front he was continuing a policy of withdrawal pivoting on the high ground north of Salerno and leaving behind him demolitions on the widest scale.

The scope of the Allied plan of campaign had developed considerably since the original landings at Reggio. As a result of the opposition at Salerno, Eighth Army had been brought up to the Potenza area at great speed, far indeed from the original objectives necessary to secure the Straits of Messina. In addition, landings had been made at Taranto, which were now linked with Eighth Army, so that a wide front had been established across southern Italy. There was

164

however no hope of the sudden collapse of German resistance and, for the time being, the co-belligerency of Italy seemed unlikely to affect the situation militarily.

The problem now, therefore, was to build up a firm front and secure the Foggia airfields and the port of Naples. The airfields round Foggia represented the most valuable objective in southern Italy, for their acquisition would give us bases from which our strategic air forces could carry the bombing offensive to industrial plants in Austria and to the oilfields in Roumania, both of which were then beyond the regular range of escorted attack.

In the development of Eighth Army's operations into the Plain of Foggia the major factor was administration. It was clearly necessary to switch my administrative axis from Calabria to the ports in south-east Italy, of which the most important were Taranto, Brindisi, and Bari. This was a major undertaking requiring considerable time and the allocation of the necessary resources. Taranto was largely occupied with troop convoys and Brindisi could not be opened before 27 September. It became apparent that I would not be able to operate my main forces north of the line Bari–Altamura–Potenza before 1 October.

The second major problem now confronting me was the regrouping of my forces in order to transfer the main weight of the Army to the east flank. I could not do this until the Salerno front was definitely secure, so I consulted General Clark on 24 September, when he agreed that my regrouping could start at once.

My plan was to advance on Foggia with 13 Corps, consisting of 1 Canadian and 78 Divisions, 4 Armoured and 1 Canadian Tank Brigades. 78 Division, as it arrived by sea, was to concentrate in the Bari area. 5 Division would initially be under command of 13 Corps but would remain in the Potenza area as the pivot of manoeuvre and link between 13 Corps and Fifth United States Army. When 13 Corps reached the general line Barletta–Melfi, 5 Division would change to command of 5 Corps, which I intended

165

THE INVASION OF ITALY   MAP 15

AND THE ADVANCE TO THE RIVER SANGRO

10 5 0   10   20   30   40   50
MILES

N

GARGANO
PENINSULA

FOGGIA   78 DIV
BARLETTA
S ANDRIA   78 DIV
CANOSA   (5 CORPS)   BARI   78 DIV
LT   LT
FORCES   FORCES
MELFI   SPINAZZOLA
LT
FORCES   GRAVINA   ALTAMURA
LT
FORCES   MATERA   BRINDISI
13   LT FORCES
CORPS   GINOSA
LETTA   TARANTO

1 A B DIV

ASTROVILLARI
SPEZZANO
CARIATI
1 CDN DIV
SAVELLI
S GIOVANNI
BELVEDERE
CROTONE
FORCES
NICASTRO
CATANZARO
GULF OF
S EUFEMIA   CDN DIV   GULF OF
231 BDE   SQUILLACE
PIZZO
5 DIV
CDO LANDING   GIOIA TAUR
1 CDN DIV
B DIV
BOVA MARINA
CAIRO
MELITO

STO

LEGEND
EIGHTH ARMY
FIFTH US ARMY
SALERNO
BRIDGEHEAD
ALL GROUND
OVER 600 METRES

initially to leave in reserve in the Taranto area with 8 Indian and 1 Airborne Divisions. Subsequently 5 Corps would be stepped forward in rear of 13 Corps to protect the left flank.

Regrouping began on 25 September, but meanwhile light forces were operating well ahead of their main bodies, although there was no way of avoiding the delay imposed by the change of administrative axis and the necessity to establish stocks of all kinds in the new base area. Even by waiting until 1 October before advancing beyond Bari, I could not avoid a further pause on the line Termoli—Campobasso—Vinchiaturo, since there were no reserve stocks in the country and the whole administrative machine required time to build up and adjust itself to the new plan of operations. The switch of base to the Taranto area and development of major operations along the east coast of Italy had not been envisaged, and advance arrangements had not been made to install the necessary resources now so much in demand.

OPERATIONS BY LIGHT FORCES BETWEEN 20 September AND 1 October

My orders to 13 Corps on reaching the Potenza—Auletta line provided for the despatch of light forces and reconnaissance elements to clear up any remaining enemy south of the line Altamura—Gravina—Potenza, then to push forward to Spinazzola and Melfi. Meanwhile 5 Corps was to continue aggressive patrolling northwards along the coast axis. The enemy covering Altamura withdrew under the combined pressure of 1 Airborne and 1 Canadian Divisions on 23 September, and our patrols pushed north through Spinazzola and reached Canosa three days later. In the coastal sector, elements of 78 Division together with some detachments of 4 Armoured Brigade landed at Bari on 22/23 September, and at once moved north to make contact with enemy rearguards at Barletta and Andria. Resistance was quickly overcome and patrols reached the Ofanto River on 24 September. After some delay due to demolitions, the advance was resumed through Foggia, which had been abandoned by the enemy on 27 September. By 1 October the Gargarno peninsula had been reported clear, but there were indications that the enemy was preparing to stand and fight in the hills north and west of the Foggia Plain.

On 1 October 13 Corps crossed the general line Barletta–Canosa, directed initially on the lateral road Termoli–Vinchiaturo. Once established firmly on this important lateral route, Eighth Army would recover the Plain of Foggia and its airfields and our immediate objective would be secured. At the Termoli line I would in any case be compelled to halt for maintenance reasons but my orders were to continue the advance as quickly as possible to secure the lateral road Pescara–Popili–Avezzano, in order to out-flank Rome. The capture of Rome, though of little military importance, was stated to be of great political significance and the city now became the next main Allied objective.

My orders to 13 Corps were that the advance to the Termoli line would be conducted on a two divisional front, 78 Division following the axis of the main coast road, while 1 Canadian Division advanced into the mountains to Vinchiaturo. Once established at Vinchiaturo the Canadians would be able to operate westwards towards Naples in co-operation with Fifth Army if by then the city had not fallen. 5 Corps was instructed to move behind 13 Corps ready to protect its west flank and rear—a necessary precaution as firm contact between Fifth and Eighth Armies was not easy to maintain in the high mountains. The positioning of 5 Corps was very important, as preservation of balance depended upon it. I laid down that as 13 Corps went for-ward 5 Division should be advanced to the Foggia area and that 4 Armoured Brigade (which was to pass to command of 5 Corps on reaching Termoli) should be positioned astride the Foggia–Naples lateral road. The Airborne Division was to stay in the general area Barletta–Andria–Canosa, while 8 Indian Division was located between Bari and Barletta.

The Desert Air Force planned to move up to the Foggia area as soon as possible.

The advance of 13 Corps started well. The enemy was known to have positions on the line of the River Biferno covering the small port of Termoli and, since the country greatly favoured the defence, plans were made to secure Termoli quickly by landings on the coast behind the enemy. On the night 2/3 October commando forces landed near the town, with the object of securing it in advance of the 78 Division thrust along the coast road. Complete surprise was achieved and the commandos secured the port and linked up with the bridgehead which was successfully established over the Biferno. Initial success was followed up by landing a brigade of 78 Division in the Termoli bridgehead on the following night.

The enemy reaction, however, was very speedy. 16 Panzer Division was rushed over from the front opposing Fifth Army, arrived during the night 3/4 October, and during the next three days launched a number of strong attacks against both the Termoli bridgehead and our forces which had crossed the river south of the town. On 5 October the enemy was fighting in Termoli itself and the flooded river prevented the passage of our tanks to assist in the battle, but by the end of the following day the bridgehead over the Biferno was firm. By 7 October the situation in the Termoli bridgehead had been restored, following the landing there of an additional brigade of 78 Division.

The enemy disengaged and fell back to positions covering the River Trigno, which were held by 16 Panzer Division (by now very depleted), and elements from 26 Panzer and 1 Parachute Divisions. As anticipated, delays were imposed by maintenance considerations and we were unable to follow up in strength until the administrative situation had been improved.

Meanwhile the Canadians were experiencing strong opposition in the difficult mountainous country and progress was slow. By 3 October they were only some 15 miles from

Vinchiaturo, but the capture of the village took several days. This thrust was now diverging from the line of advance of 78 Division and I decided to bring forward another division to fill the gap between the two axes. This decision involved regrouping, for the front was becoming too wide for one corps to control and I ordered 5 Corps to take over the coastal sector with 78 Division, while 13 Corps was instructed to operate inland on a front of two divisions—1 Canadian and 5 Divisions.

2 New Zealand Division was due to be concentrated in the Taranto area by 15 November and this I decided to hold initially in Army reserve.

By 11 October, Eighth Army was established at Termoli and Vinchiaturo and the Foggia airfields were safeguarded; my forces were regrouping and once again major operations awaited the administrative adjustments which were being made in the rear areas.

THE SITUATION IN EIGHTH ARMY ON REACHING THE TERMOLI—VINCHIATURO LINE

Having secured the Foggia airfields, Eighth Army was given the task of advancing to the 'Rome Line', which was the name given to the lateral road Pescara—Avezzano—Rome. There were two major factors confronting me in planning the development of my operations: administrative considerations and the weather.

I have explained already that our advance from Reggio was continually delayed by maintenance difficulties. Administration had not been able to keep pace with operational planning and this was now to have serious consequences, for the winter weather was beginning. Obviously our difficulties were going to be greatly increased when winter conditions set in, because the 'leg' of Italy is essentially ideal defensive country and when climatic conditions operated in the enemy's favour, it might become almost impregnable. The Adriatic winter is severe; seaborne operations would be uncertain; on land progress would become impossible off

171

the main roads owing to snow and mud; mountain torrents subject to violent fluctuations would create great bridging difficulties and flying would be constantly restricted by low cloud and mist.

Rome was the immediate Allied objective and it was increasingly certain that unless we could secure the city very rapidly, weather would undoubtedly impose long delays on our plans. At the same time, our difficulties were immeasurably increased by a change in the enemy's conduct of the campaign, for it became apparent from his resistance at Salerno, Vinchiaturo, and Termoli that his withdrawal policy had been superseded. The Allied advance along the whole front was now being solidly contested and reports showed that the German forces in Italy were being reinforced and had reached a total of some twenty-four divisions.

RESUMPTION OF THE ADVANCE FROM THE
TERMOLI—VINCHIATURO LINE

During the middle of October our preparations were proceeding for the resumption of the advance in strength. At the same time on Fifth Army front the River Volturno had been crossed but the enemy resistance continued to be very strong and further reinforcement of the front opposite Eighth Army had also been established. We had now four German divisions facing us—16 and 26 Panzer, 29 Panzer Grenadier, and 1 Parachute Divisions grouped together as 76 Panzer Corps.

After the fall of Termoli operations on a limited scale continued with the object of squaring up to the defences on the River Trigno, but I had to wait until 21 October before commencing really strong efforts to get into close contact with the enemy positions. My outline plan for breaching the Trigno defences was based on diversionary operations on the western flank, followed by a strong thrust up the coast. In order to focus the enemy's attention inland I intended that 13 Corps should deliver a strong attack on the axis Vinchiaturo—Isernia prior to the 5 Corps operations on the

172

river, and set a target date of 28 October for the thrust. On the night 30/31 October 5 Corps would attack across the Trigno with 8 Indian and 78 Divisions. Providing the weather held, I did not anticipate great difficulty in crossing the river, but further north the enemy was preparing a major defensive system based on the River Sangro. I therefore gave orders that once the 5 Corps operation started it would be carried through to the Sangro position, as we should probably need a pause there in order to study the opposition and launch a full scale attack. At the same time I ordered 2 New Zealand Division forward to the Foggia area to preserve balance in my dispositions and to provide a safeguard for the Foggia airfields.

During the pause energetic patrolling on 5 Corps front achieved considerable local success and on the night 22/23 October 78 Division got a battalion across the Trigno River. On the south bank the ground descended steeply to end in a bluff which made crossing operations difficult; on the north bank there was a plain some two miles wide leading to the San Salvo ridge along which the main enemy positions were disposed. Preliminary operations aimed at establishing forces in the plain, but from this time forward the offensive on all sectors began to be affected seriously by heavy and continuous rain. Efforts to increase the 78 Division bridge-head over the Trigno on 27 and 28 October were foiled by the mud and wet, while 13 Corps attack towards Isernia had to be postponed. Eventually 5 Division of 13 Corps started off in the pouring rain on the night 29/30 October and, in spite of the weather, difficult country, and demolitions, succeeded in capturing Cantalupo on 31 October. Progress on this flank met increasing difficulties and the enemy resistance appeared to have been further strengthened; his tactics were now based on fortifying the very strongly built mountain villages which became formidable to capture; and when forced to withdraw, he destroyed existing accommodation in the villages so that the attacking troops would find little shelter in them.

After a number of postponements because of the down-pour, 5 Corps launched the main thrust across the river on the night 2/3 November. A heavy artillery programme and naval gunfire supported the assault and good progress was made during the night in spite of firm resistance. During 3 November heavy fighting went on, particularly round San Salvo station where our troops were counter attacked by enemy tanks. Operations continued on the second night, during which an interesting incident occurred when an infantry battalion advanced into a German tank leaguer; intense confusion followed, but as a result the German armour in the sector withdrew a considerable distance. On the morning of 4 November the enemy was found to have started pulling back on the whole 5 Corps front. Troops of 78 Division passed through Vasto on the following day and continued the advance towards the Sangro. On their left 8 Indian Division took Palmoli and reached the lateral road to Vasto and had soon cleared down to the area of Torrebruna. By then 13 Corps, after considerable delays due mainly to demolitions, had captured Isernia. I was careful to ensure that no gap occurred between the two Corps thrusts and gave orders that reconnaissance troops were to be used for patrolling between the main axes of advance.

By 8 November 78 Division was on the high ground overlooking the River Sangro on a two brigade front, with 8 Indian Division coming up on its left. Preparations for tackling the Sangro position were now initiated.

REFLECTIONS ON THE SITUATION AS WE APPROACHED THE SANGRO

The conduct of operations was still suffering from the frustration due to lack of resources, which made it impossible to develop the desired strength and speed of action. The possibility of the Allies' securing Rome quickly was now remote. The build-up of our forces in Italy was being retarded by the withdrawal of craft and shipping in preparation for the North West European campaign and, since

174

there were insufficient Allied resources to fight two major campaigns, it was no longer to be expected that spectacular results could be achieved in Italy quickly. This factor, combined with the enormous difficulties of campaigning in ideally defensive country in severe winter conditions, together with the strengthening of the enemy opposition, argued that from a strictly military point of view the continuance of the offensive during the winter would be unjustified. It was considered, however, desirable for other reasons that we should get Rome: but the problem of securing this objective was becoming increasingly formidable. At the beginning of November Eighth Army still had many of its units in Africa and it was becoming clear that we should not reach the Pescara Line with four infantry divisions only: I required at least one more. My troops were getting very tired and my formations had suffered considerable casualties since the landings at Reggio. In particular the officer situation in the infantry had become acute.

CHAPTER SEVENTEEN

THE BATTLE OF THE RIVER SANGRO,
28 NOVEMBER 1943

PRELIMINARY OPERATIONS

In conformity with his policy of holding the Allied advance, the enemy on our front had undertaken the construction of the 'Winter Line', a very strong natural position based on the River Sangro and strengthened by defence works. The Sangro was in flood, the level of water being subject to wide variation according to the amount of rain falling in the mountains, but with very great difficulty it could be forded at certain periods. On the south bank of the river there is an escarpment. On the north a low lying plain extends to a steep sided ridge along which the main enemy positions were located, and to which I shall refer in this narrative as the Sangro Ridge. The main bastions of the enemy defensive system on the ridge were the two villages of Mozzagrogna and Fossacesia.

I had of course been considering the methods of tackling the Sangro position while we were on the River Trigno. The time factor made it important for me to manoeuvre the Army during the advance from the Trigno to the Sangro in a way which would ensure minimum delay in getting to grips with the problem of piercing the 'Winter Line'; we were running what was to prove a losing race with the winter weather.

There were three alternatives for the Sangro battle. First, to attack on the left flank with 13 Corps astride Castel di Sangro on the two roads leading north to the Pescara–Avezzano lateral. Here we should be faced with difficulties in the high mountains, where the roads are liable to be blocked by snowdrifts; at best only one division could operate on each road and they would not be mutually supporting because of lack of lateral communications across the high central massif. In short, a powerful offensive on the left flank was hardly possible in the winter months, for apart from the operational limitations there would be great maintenance problems and the conditions of cloud and mist in the mountains would virtually preclude the use of our air power.

Secondly, there was the possibility of an attack in the central sector of 5 Corps front astride the roads from Atessa to Casoli and Castel Frentano. It would have been difficult if not impossible, however, to mount a major attack on this axis because of the extremely poor communications south of the river. But it gave quick access to the lateral road to the west from San Vito, which ran behind the Sangro River, and would therefore be useful for establishing a threat to the enemy's defences.

Thirdly, on the coastal axis a possible thrust line was through Fossacesia to Lanciano and San Vito thence northwards to Pescara and Chieti. An attack on this axis would have a good main road and could be prepared and mounted quickly with full artillery support. In the coastal plain the air forces would operate in the best available conditions and warships too could co-operate from the sea.

I therefore decided to deliver a strong blow on the coastal sector with 8 Indian and 78 Divisions with the object of breaking into the enemy defences on the Sangro Ridge on a narrow front. The troops were then to work outwards from the area of penetration. In order to increase the power of the offensive I decided to bring 2 New Zealand Division up on the left of 5 Corps to mount a strong threat along the road axis running north from Atessa. If operations went well this division could be pushed through to an area west of Chieti on the Rome lateral, ready to turn west directed on Popoli and Avezzano. If it were in any way possible to get this division to Avezzano the problem of helping Fifth Army forward towards Rome would be simplified. Meanwhile 5

Corps would advance along the main coast road to Pescara and Chieti with the ultimate object of establishing a bridge-head north of the Pescara River.

At a conference held at Army Group Headquarters on 8 November, I explained my plan for piercing the 'Winter Line' and my proposal for the subsequent development of operations. It was agreed that Fifth United States Army would continue pressure on its front so as to pin down the enemy and assist the development of the Eighth Army's plan to establish our troops in the Avezzano area.

ORDERS FOR THE ATTACK ON THE WINTER LINE

My detailed orders for the attack over the River Sangro were based on achieving surprise by deceiving the enemy as to the direction of my main thrust. I intended to continue attempts to divert the enemy's attention to my western flank so I now ordered 13 Corps to operate strongly to secure the area Castel Alfedena and later Roccaraso. At the same time I asked Fifth United States Army to co-operate by increasing its activity on my western flank. These operations were to commence at once and would have the effect of breaking into the southern end of the Sangro position. Meanwhile 5 Corps was to close up to the Sangro line and prepare to launch the main attack which would be delivered by 8 Indian and 78 Divisions together with 4 Armoured Brigade.

My plan involved relieving 8 Indian Division on the left sector of 5 Corps front by 2 New Zealand Division, then concentrating the former behind 78 Division ready for the assault on a very narrow front. These moves had to be kept from the Germans and with this object a brigade of 8 Indian Division was to remain on the New Zealand front until the last minute. The target date for the attack by 5 Corps was 20 November and the first main objective was the general line Ortona–Lanciano.

Thenceforward the weather rapidly deteriorated. Heavy rain frequently continued for two days, only to be followed by one or two further days of drizzle and mist. Snow was falling in the mountains and the state of the roads and country became wet and very muddy. At least 48 hours' dry weather was necessary before the country became passable after a wet spell and in these circumstances the plan was subjected to continual postponements. Eventually it became necessary to modify the plan itself.

During the period 9–15 November 78 Division succeeded in crossing the river and in establishing a small bridgehead on the north bank from which battle patrols operated forward to the escarpment. Our identifications showed that the Germans opposing 78 Division belonged to 65 Infantry Division, which had horse transport. Behind it was 15 Panzer Grenadier Division, believed to be very weak in tanks. All we needed therefore was a spell of fine weather in order to exploit our superiority over the enemy, but the rain was persistent and the level of the Sangro repeatedly varied by as much as six or seven feet in a day as a result of downpours in the mountains. The mud and slush became truly appalling.

I had to postpone the date of the attack, and decided that I should have to modify the scope of my plan. In the prevailing weather conditions it did not seem feasible to launch a major breakthrough operation which would carry us straight to the Pescara line. As a first phase we could not hope to do more than take quick advantage of a dry spell to secure the Sangro Ridge. Once the enemy was denied observation over the river, bridging could be started, roads and tracks built up and the general movement problem across the valley properly organized. We would then be able to continue our advance northwards. In short, the weather forced me to adopt a policy of advancing by short methodical stages between which communications could be established and demolitions and obstacles overcome.

I ordered 5 Corps to build up the strength of the bridgehead in the river plain, preparatory to attacking the ridge. This involved sacrificing some of the measures taken to

179

achieve surprise and I therefore ordered 2 New Zealand Division to get patrols across the Sangro, in order to increase the pressure on the enemy and to broaden the front.

In accordance with my new policy five battalions were established on the north bank of the river by 22 November, but further rain then brought us again to a complete standstill.

It looked as if we would have an indefinite time to wait before an operation could be launched which involved the use of large numbers of tanks, and I came to the conclusion that I would have to devise further modifications to the plan in order to make it independent of tanks and of weather. I instructed 5 Corps to reorganize the bridgehead on a two divisional basis, bringing 8 Indian Division up on the left of 78 Division and to plan the capture of the Sangro River by a series of very limited operations each supported by the whole Corps artillery. Before dawn on 26 November an attack would be mounted to secure the enemy localities halfway up the ridge towards San Maria. Two days later a further attack would be delivered against San Maria and Mozzagrogna, and subsequently 78 Division would operate from San Maria in a north-easterly direction towards Fossacesia in order to clear the ridge. If the mud and wet precluded tank attacks, these thrusts were within the capability of the infantry alone and were to be carried through with fierce determination.

By 24 November I had a very firm bridgehead north of the River Sangro about 2,000 yards deep on a frontage of 10,000 yards. This was a very fine performance on the part of the infantry and sappers. Meanwhile, New Zealand patrols were active across the river in their sector and the south bank had been cleared of enemy throughout its length. In connection with 5 Corps attack on 28 November, the New Zealand Division was ordered to launch an assault across the river at the same time on a two brigade front. Meanwhile 13 Corps operations on the western flank continued and on 24 November Castel Alfedena was taken and held in face of strong counter attacks.

By 27 November all was ready for the battle. It was a fine dry day and 100 tanks of 4 Armoured Brigade, many carriers, and much transport were got across to the north bank. Throughout the day the enemy positions were heavily bombed. On the New Zealand sector our troops closed up to the river and worked hard on improving communications to the front. If the weather held it was probable that armoured units would be able to accompany the infantry in their attacks along the ridge and this would, of course, accelerate the rolling up of the hostile defences from the flanks and rear. Very heavy artillery support was available and, weather permitting, a great weight of air power. I anticipated that once we got on to the ridge and captured Mozzagrogna and San Maria, we should have a 'dog-fight' which might well last two days before we completed the capture of 5 Corps objectives.

The weather on 28 November was fine and the assault began at 2130 hours. 8 Indian Division captured Mozzagrogna quickly, but demolitions prevented tanks and supporting weapons getting forward and ground had to be sacrificed in face of a German counter attack at dawn. On the left, 2 New Zealand Division went well and secured its initial objectives, together with a good bridgehead over the river by first light 29 November. Throughout the day heavy fighting continued round Mozzagrogna where the enemy was using tanks and flame-throwers, but during the night 28/29 November the village was captured and 4 Armoured Brigade got through the place by midday. Tanks and infantry, having got on to the ridge, began to turn outwards in order to clear it and experienced intense fighting, but our progress was greatly facilitated by the magnificent scale of air support. It was clear towards the end of 29 November that we had broken into the enemy's 'Winter Line', and I

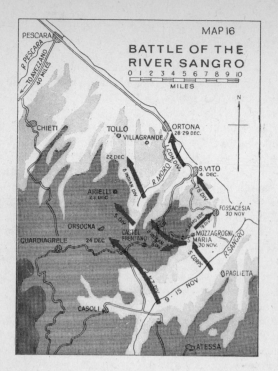

BATTLE OF THE
RIVER SANGRO

0 1 2 3 4 5 6 7 8 9 10
MILES

MAP 16

ordered 5 Corps to continue operations on 30 November in
two directions: 78 Division was to clear Fossacesia and then
move north-west towards San Vito; 8 Indian Division was to
operate from Mozzagrogna along the ridge towards Castel
Frentano. It was important to give the enemy no let-up as
the full brunt of our attack had fallen on 65 Infantry
Division: which had received a great hammering and was
now very unsteady.

During 30 November 4 Armoured Brigade took
Fossacesia supported by a heavy artillery barrage and 8
Indian Division, after beating off a counter attack by 26
Panzer Division at Mozzagrogna, worked along the ridge
and captured the high ground overlooking Castel Frentano.

182

Meanwhile the New Zealanders, having overcome great difficulties in establishing a river crossing and approaches to it, were expanding their bridgehead. By dark the whole ridge overlooking the River Sangro, which was the backbone of the 'Winter Line', was in our hands, and the 5 Corps and New Zealand bridgeheads had linked up to form one deep penetration of the enemy defensive system. 1,000 prisoners and much equipment were captured. My orders on 1 December provided for the establishment of a firm base on the vital Sangro Ridge, while limited thrusts were launched on the two flanks. I instructed 5 Corps not to send main bodies beyond the line of the lateral road San Vito–Lanciano until communications across the Sangro had been made storm-proof and flood-proof. 78 Division with 4 Armoured Brigade was to secure San Vito and send light forces ahead towards Ortona. 8 Indian Division with the Canadian Tank Brigade (which I now brought forward) was to form the firm base on the ridge. I also ordered 2 New Zealand Division to push forward to secure Castel Frentano, Guardiagrele and Orsogna. In order to cover the gap between the New Zealanders and 13 Corps, I ordered forward a Parachute brigade with a regiment of airborne artillery, which was to operate under command of the New Zealand Division. The layout of the front was now well organized, but we needed good weather to exploit our victory. My object was to push one division along the coast road to Ortona and later on if possible to Pescara, while a second progressed on the inland axis towards Chieti. 78 Division was now very tired and I gave orders for its relief by 1 Canadian Division which was to be brought across from 13 Corps. 13 Corps now could have little but a holding role, for which only one division was required in the line, and 78 Division, after relief, would go into reserve in 13 Corps area. By 4 December 5 Corps had captured San Vito and Lanciano but was held up on the line of the River Moro, and 2 New Zealand Division had faced up to Orsogna and Guardiagrele. Operations were now again delayed by rain, but by 6 December the high level bridge across the River Sangro at Paglieta had been completed.

The enemy resistance was very determined along the whole front. Our moves were subject to strong and repeated counter attacks, particularly in the New Zealand sector where, in addition to 26 Panzer Division and some parachute battalions, 65 Infantry Division had been brought back into the line after a brief respite. 5 Corps was now opposed by 90 Panzer Grenadier Division, which had started arriving on our front on 1 December. Away on the left flank 13 Corps was opposed by one parachute division only, and since any offensive in the mountains was out of the question, I decided to regroup my divisions with the object of strengthening the right flank further. I therefore ordered Headquarters 13 Corps with 5 Division to come across to the coastal sector, leaving 78 Division to hold the mountain flank directly under Army command. I proposed to continue my drive to the north on a frontage of two Corps: on the right 5 Corps with 1 Canadian and 8 Indian Divisions and on the left 13 Corps with 2 New Zealand and 5 Divisions.

By 10 December 1 Canadian Division had secured a bridgehead over the River Moro and pushed on towards Ortona, in spite of numerous counter attacks in which very heavy casualties were inflicted on the enemy. The Desert Air Force was doing splendid work and co-operation from warships was also proving most valuable. I instructed 5 Corps to swing 8 Indian Division up towards Tollo on the left flank of the Canadians and accelerated the leading brigade of 5 Division now moving round to the coastal sector with 13 Corps, so that I could order it into the line between 2 New Zealand and 8 Indian Divisions. The opposition at Orsogna and Guardiagrele was still very sticky for the two villages had been converted into major strong points, and their location on dominating ground made them very difficult of approach. The ground floors and cellars of the houses had been strengthened and in them the enemy garrison withstood repeated air attacks.

My long term policy remained to secure the Pescara–Chieti lateral and then to develop operations towards Rome. My plan involved driving forward on a front of two Corps with the object of establishing a bridgehead over the Pescara River with 1 Canadian Division on the right and 5 Division on the left. 8 Indian Division would pass into reserve between Pescara and Chieti while the New Zealanders, having advanced through Guardiagrele to Chieti, would turn southwest to Avezzano. Owing to the difficulty of the Guardiagrele–Chieti road axis, I intended to advance 5 Corps ahead of 13 Corps in order to threaten the communications of the enemy troops in the general area of Orsogna. This would facilitate the progress of 13 Corps and the New Zealanders.

Meanwhile, the enemy was known to be sending further reinforcements to the Eighth Army front and we heard of the expected arrival of 334 Infantry Division from Genoa. This was the third division which the Germans had sent to reinforce his eastern flank since the beginning of the Sangro battle, the others being 90 PG Division from Venice and 26 Panzer Division from the Fifth United States Army front.

5 Corps operations against Ortona continued relentlessly against desperate enemy resistance. The Canadians got into the outskirts of the town on 20 December, but it took a week to clear it owing to the remarkably tenacious fighting of the German paratroop garrison. The Canadian troops were quite magnificent and in the end outfought the Germans.

Meanwhile 8 Indian Division continued its operations towards Tollo and succeeded in taking Villa Grandi on 22 December.

In 13 Corps, the plan to assault Orsogna was eventually dropped as it would have proved very costly. Instead, operations were developed to outflank the enemy's defences to the north and by 24 December the New Zealanders had captured the high ground to the north-east of the town.

Between 2 New Zealand and 8 Indian Divisions, 5 Division captured Arielli on 23 December.

This was the general situation on the front of Eighth Army at the close of 1943 when I was ordered to hand over my command and return to fresh tasks in England.

SOME REFLECTIONS ON THE CAMPAIGN IN ITALY

The original Allied object in invading Italy was to knock that country out of the war. This was achieved very soon after our leading troops had landed on the mainland.

Following the Armistice there had been a hope that to evict the Germans from Italy with the aid of the Italian Army would be a speedy matter. Events proved this impossible and we became involved in a major campaign lacking a pre-determined plan of action. The result was that the administrative machine became unable to keep pace with the constantly widening scope of our operational commitments. We were therefore unable to exploit our advantages in September and October, when operationally a speedy advance to the 'Rome Line' seemed still a very feasible proposition. If then we had had the resources to allow us to maintain pressure on the enemy, our superiority in armour and in the air might have enabled us to roll the enemy back to the 'Rome Line' before the winter began.

By the time the Allies had secured Naples and the Foggia airfields the bad weather was upon us. If the capture of Rome was then considered an urgent necessity, it could have been ensured only by the allocation of sufficient resources to build up the Armies and their immediately associated Air Forces to a strength adequate for the task. By then, however, other considerations were involved; craft and shipping were removed in preparation for the Western European front, and local import facilities were restricted by the demands of the Strategic Air Forces which were being established at Foggia. We could not do everything at once.

The tempo of the land operations in Italy therefore decreased and the capture of Rome became increasingly difficult. In three months the Allies had captured Sicily, knocked Italy out of the war, locked up the Italian fleet in Malta and secured Naples and the Foggia airfields. These were spectacular gains. Thereafter it was necessary to reduce the resources made available for the land forces. And, since this coincided with increased enemy resistance and the advent of winter, we could no longer hope for quick results.

CHAPTER EIGHTEEN

ADMINISTRATION IN THE CAMPAIGN IN ITALY

Throughout Part Three I have had to say repeatedly that my operations were hampered by administrative difficulties. In the immediately preceding paragraphs, in which I gave my reflections on the campaign, I indicated the reason. We became involved in a major campaign without having made in advance the administrative plans and arrangements necessary to sustain the impetus of our operations.

It may be of interest to explain rather more fully what this lack of previous planning involved.

Sound administrative arrangements had been made to maintain the Eighth Army, with its two Corps in Sicily. When Operation 'Baytown' was launched on 3 September across the Straits of Messina, the administrative build-up was incomplete; a proportion of the units and supplies intended to complete it was subsequently delivered but others were diverted to the 'Avalanche' operation at Salerno. The complete priority awarded to the Fifth United States Army absorbed such reserves of administrative resources as were immediately available in the Mediterranean. The operation launched at Taranto by 5 Corps was prepared at short notice and the scale of administrative support allotted to it was of the slenderest: reliance in the first instance being placed on assistance from the Italians both as to supplies and transport.

The effect of these circumstances was that a reinforced Eighth Army had to be supported in Italy by something less than the administrative resources which had been provided for its operations in Sicily. But stores and transport collected in Sicily could not be suddenly spirited into Italy. Rail communications did not exist. Roads were long and heavily demolished and the ferry at Messina could handle only a small volume of traffic.

The further stores convoys which were scheduled for Sicily were diverted to the 'heel' ports of Italy, but these ships had been loaded in bulk on the assumption that their cargoes would be used to stock up the depots in Sicily where a small balanced stock had already been accumulated. Their arrival in the 'heel' ports did not help the situation very materially; the Eighth Army, having just based itself on Taranto and Brindisi wanted certain things only, and wanted them badly. The capacity of the ports was strictly limited and they were faced with the problem of discharging large quantities of stores, useless for the moment, in order to extract the vital stores which were needed so badly.

The switch of my administrative axis from Calabria to the 'heel' ports was, from an administrative point of view, the crisis of the campaign. It must be remembered that I 'drove' the Eighth Army forward into the Potenza area at great speed in order to assist the operation at Salerno. In doing so I had been fully warned by my staff that I was taking big administrative risks. The advice was sound, just as I consider that my decision to ignore it was sound. The risks were real and, although I succeeded in my tactical objective to relieve the enemy pressure on the Fifth United States Army, I paid the penalty of finding that my own reserves were exhausted and that a flow of supplies to replenish them was not forthcoming. Had all this been foreseen, adequate supplies might already have arrived in the 'heel' ports and my administrative situation could have been re-adjusted. But there was no pre-determined plan and a crisis occurred; it could not quickly be overcome and right up to the end of my operations in Italy its effects continued to be felt: though in an ever lessening degree.

Our administrative difficulties were not confined to shortage of ordinary supplies such as rations and petrol. Equally important was the difficulty in maintaining the efficiency of

189

our transport. In describing the Sicilian campaign I have mentioned that it had been decided, and rightly, not to establish in Sicily base workshops or base ordnance depots. Soon after the campaign on the Italian mainland had been started it was decided to establish advanced ordnance depots at Naples and Bari. Owing to the time which it takes to set up depots of this description, the benefit from them was hardly felt during my period of command in Italy. This was a circumstance which could not have been avoided given the conditions in which the Italian campaign was launched. With regard to base workshops it was planned that the repair of engine assemblies should continue to be done in the base workshops in Egypt. There was grave difficulty about moving these workshops, not the least of which was that they employed a very large number of local artisans. The distances, however, that separated my troops from these workshops in Egypt was such that a satisfactory turn-round could not be established whereby unserviceable assemblies could be promptly replaced. For these reasons my transport resources became progressively weaker just at the time when I had most need of them.

A new feature in the Italian campaign was the heavy rate of ammunition expenditure. Experience gained in the desert proved rather deceptive in this respect. The Sicilian campaign had not lasted long enough to bring the matter of ammunition expenditure into prominence. The Battle of the Sangro was the first real warning given to us that in close and easily defended country we could expect a need for ammunition on a scale far higher than that to which we had been accustomed.

The capture of the Foggia airfields immediately gave rise to heavy demands for supplies for the Strategic Air Force. The obvious point of entry for these supplies was Bari. In these circumstances the three 'heel' ports between them could not meet the combined demands of Eighth Army and the Air Force. There was surplus port capacity available at Naples where the United States Engineers had accomplished a remarkable achievement in repairing the very heavy damage. The extent, however, to which Naples could be used immediately to satisfy my requirements was limited. In the first place it involved a diversion of shipping which can seldom be accomplished without some loss of time. Secondly, the only rail communications available between the Bay of Naples and the Adriatic was a difficult single line track via Potenza and Taranto.

The plan which had been made for the developing of the port of Naples aimed at using it for the Fifth United States Army consisting of one United States Corps and one British Corps. The fact that British as well as American supplies had to be handled at Naples, and that supplies for the United States Air Corps as well as for the British Eighth Army had to be handled in the 'heel' ports, demanded a close co-ordination between the administrative arrangements of the two Allies. Headquarters Fortbase, which had been responsible for organizing my rear administration in Sicily, was set up in Taranto at the end of September to fill the same role on behalf of Eighth Army in Italy. The Peninsula Base Section, which fulfilled the corresponding role for the American troops in the Fifth United States Army, was established about the same time in Naples. It was urgently necessary to co-ordinate the working of these two staffs. The decision taken was to close down Headquarters Fortbase, to transfer the staff to Naples and to reconstitute it there on a strengthened basis as an advanced administrative echelon of Allied Force Headquarters. Its responsibilities for local administration on the Lines of Communication were trans-ferred to a District Headquarters under its command. This advanced administrative echelon was then given authority to co-ordinate on the spot all administrative arrangements, British and United States, in Italy. In particular it was given power to control the acceptance of cargoes at all ports, to allocate rail capacity and to lay down priorities for railway repairs. The officer in charge of this advanced echelon Headquarters was also appointed as administrative staff officer to General Alexander, who simultaneously dispensed with his own administrative staff. This change in organization was beneficial and its effects were quickly felt in the Eighth Army. A further change was made in December when the command of this administrative staff passed to Headquarters 15 Army Group, so that it became in name, as well as in fact, the administrative portion of 15 Army Group staff. This revision to a more normal arrangement was completed when General Alexander concentrated his Headquarters, both operational and administrative, at Caserta in January 1944.

I have mentioned these various changes which took place in the administrative organization in rear of Eighth Army partly because they had a very definite effect on my maintenance position, and partly because they concern the problem to which I have been referring in previous chapters: namely the problem of administrative control. The American method of solving this problem is a straightforward one. The Army Commander controls administration within his own area. The lines of communication in rear are controlled by the Services of Supply. I think that our own system is more flexible, but for that very reason it sometimes tends to become complicated. An administrative organization should be simple. It should normally ensure that the commander of a formation has control of an area extending back to the point at which his supplies are mainly delivered. Normally, in the case of an Army, this is a group of railheads but it may, as in the desert, be a port. In the case of an Army Group, the Army Group Commander will normally control a series of ports at which his supplies are delivered from overseas. If more than one Army Group is involved a GHQ must be set up to control the Base Depots and ports from which they are fed. The administrative responsibilities of the Army Group are then confined to the allotment of priorities between the demands of the various Armies, in order to ensure that available supplies are utilized in the manner which best fits the operational plan of the Army Group

Commander. These are the broad principles, in my opinion, which should decide the answer to the problem of administrative control. I agree that there should be flexibility in their application, but two conditions must always be observed. The first is that every administrative organization must be simple. The second is that every operational commander must have a degree of control over the administrative plan corresponding to the scope of his responsibilities for the operational plan.

CHAPTER NINETEEN

MY FAREWELL TO THE EIGHTH ARMY

Towards the end of December I was appointed to command Twenty-First Army Group which was then preparing in England for the invasion of Western Europe. On 31 December I handed over to my successor, Lieutenant-General Sir Oliver Leese, and took off from the Sangro airstrip for home. Before leaving I issued a farewell message to all ranks of the Eighth Army, which is reproduced in this book, and I think I can here say little more than is expressed there about my feelings at relinquishing command of this great family of fighting men.

I spent 1 January 1944 at Marrakech with the Prime Minister. Before I left for England that night, Mr Churchill wrote the following in my autograph book:

'The immortal march of the Eighth Army from the gates of Cairo along the African shore, through Sicily, has now carried its ever victorious soldiers far into Italy towards the gates of Rome. The scene changes and vastly expands. A great task accomplished gives place to a greater, in which the same unfailing spirit will win for all true men a full and glorious reward.

WINSTON S. CHURCHILL.'

EIGHTH ARMY PERSONAL MESSAGE FROM THE ARMY COMMANDER
To be read out to all troops

1. I have to tell you, with great regret, that the time has come for me to leave the Eighth Army. I have been ordered to take command of the British Armies in England that are to operate under General Eisenhower—the Supreme Commander.

2. It is difficult to express to you adequately what this parting means to me. I am leaving officers and men who have been my comrades during months of hard and victorious fighting, and whose courage and devotion to duty always filled me with admiration. I feel I have many friends among the soldiery of this great Army. I do not know if you will miss me; but I will miss you more than I can say, and especially will I miss the personal contacts, and the cheerful greetings we exchanged together when we passed each other on the road.

3. In all the battles we have fought together we have not had one single failure; we have been successful in everything we have undertaken.

I know that this has been due to the devotion to duty and whole-hearted co-operation of every officer and man, rather than to anything I may have been able to do myself.

But the result has been a mutual confidence between you and me, and mutual confidence between a Commander and his troops is a pearl of very great price.

4. I am also very sad at parting from the Desert Air Force. This magnificent air striking force has fought with the Eighth Army throughout the whole of its victorious progress; every soldier in this Army is proud to acknowledge that the support of this strong and powerful air force

195

has been a battle-winning factor of the first importance. We owe the Allied Air Forces in general, and the Desert Air Force in particular, a very great debt of gratitude.

5. What can I say to you as I go away?

When the heart is full it is not easy to speak. But I would say this to you:

'You have made this Army what it is. YOU have made its name a household word all over the world. YOU must uphold its good name and its traditions.

'And I would ask you to give to my successor the same loyal and devoted service that you have never failed to give to me.'

6. And so I say GOOD-BYE to you all.

May we meet again soon; and may we serve together again as comrades in arms in the final stages of this war.

ITALY   B. L. MONTGOMERY
1 January 1944   General, Eighth Army

COMBAT REPORT

by BILL LAMBERT

1914–1918 were years of crisis. For the first time in history war was being fought in the trenches, at sea *and* in the air. Aviation was still in its infancy, and to the pilots of World War I each flight was an adventure—a far cry from the computerized safety of today . . .

COMBAT REPORT

is Captain Bill Lambert's story of the time he spent in the famous 24 Squadron. His unshakeable love of flying helped him to become one of the most outstanding fighter pilots of the war and in this, his own personal 'combat report', he describes his most dangerous and exciting aerial victories . . .

0 552 09742 X—**50p**   T228

THE SHADOW WAR

by HENRI MICHEL

They were an army without a flag—an army whose weapons were pitifully inadequate and whose training left much to be desired. But during the Second World War they caused chaos and disruption to many of the plans and strategies of the Third Reich . . .

'They' were the Resistance fighters—small bands of ordinary working people in Scandinavia, Holland, France, Greece, and Poland who fought with everything they had towards the attainment of one single goal . . . victory over the Germans.

The Shadow War is the complete story of the brave men and women whose courage so often went unnoticed and whose operations were some of the closest-kept secrets of the war . . .

0 552 09727 6—**60p**   T229

A SELECTED LIST OF WAR BOOKS
THAT APPEAR IN CORGI

☐	09055 7	SIDESHOW	*Gerard Bell* 30p
☐	09042 5	THE LUFTWAFFE WAR DIARIES	*Cajus Bekker* 60p
☐	08512 X	THE BIG SHOW	*Pierre Clostermann D.F.C.* 40p
☐	09259 2	YELLOW PERIL	*Gilbert Hackforth-Jones* 35p
☐	09383 1	DANGEROUS TRADE	*Gilbert Hackforth-Jones* 30p
☐	09178 2	REIGN OF HELL	*Sven Hassel* 40p
☐	08874 9	SS GENERAL	*Sven Hassel* 40p
☐	08779 3	ASSIGNMENT GESTAPO	*Sven Hassel* 40p
☐	08603 7	LIQUIDATE PARIS	*Sven Hassel* 40p
☐	08528 6	MARCH BATTALION	*Sven Hassel* 40p
☐	08168 X	MONTE CASSINO	*Sven Hassel* 35p
☐	07871 9	COMRADES OF WAR	*Sven Hassel* 35p
☐	07242 7	WHEELS OF TERROR	*Sven Hassel* 40p
☐	07241 9	THE LEGION OF THE DAMNED	*Sven Hassel* 35p
☐	07470 5	THE BLUE MAX	*Jack D. Hunter* 35p
☐	09246 0	MAUTHAUSEN: HISTORY OF A DEATH CAMP	*Evelyn Le Chéne* 40p
☐	08222 8	SAGITTARIUS RISING	*Cecil Lewis* 25p
☐	08371 2	THE DIRTY DOZEN	*E. M. Mathanson* 50p
☐	09422 6	BOY IN THE BLITZ	*Colin Perry* 35p
☐	08536 7	THE SCOURGE OF THE SWASTIKA (illus.)	
			Lord Russell of Liverpool 40p
☐	08537 5	THE KNIGHTS OF BUSHIDO	*Lord Russell of Liverpool* 35p
☐	09324 6	FIGHTER EXPLOITS (illus.)	*Edward H. Sims* 40p
☐	08169 8	633 SQUADRON	*Frederick E. Smith* 35p
☐	09308 4	THE JUNGLE IS NEUTRAL	*F. Spencer Chapman* 50p
☐	09549 4	NO BANNERS	*John Oram Thomas* 40p
☐	08986 9	DUEL OF EAGLES (illus.)	*Peter Townsend* 50p
☐	09541 9	INVASION '44	*John Frayn Turner* 40p
☐	09094 2	THE LONG WATCH	*Alan White* 25p
☐	09367 X	SLAVES OF THE SON OF HEAVEN	*R. H. Whitecross* 35p

All these books are available at your bookshop or newsagent: or can be ordered direct from the publisher. Just tick the titles you want and fill in the form below.

....

CORGI BOOKS, Cash Sales Department, P.O. Box 11, Falmouth, Cornwall.
Please send cheque or postal order. No currency, and allow 10p per book to cover the cost of postage and packing (plus 5p each for additional copies).

NAME (*Block letters*)..

ADDRESS ....

(FEB. 75) ....

While every effort is made to keep prices low, it is sometimes necessary to increase prices at short notice. Corgi Books reserve the right to show new retail prices on covers which may differ from those previously advertised in the text or elsewhere.